Cambridge Elements =

Elements in the Philosophy of Mathematics
edited by
Penelope Rush
University of Tasmania
Stewart Shapiro
The Ohio State University

ITERATIVE CONCEPTIONS OF SET

Neil Barton
*National University of Singapore
and University of Oslo*

CAMBRIDGE
UNIVERSITY PRESS

Shaftesbury Road, Cambridge CB2 8EA, United Kingdom

One Liberty Plaza, 20th Floor, New York, NY 10006, USA

477 Williamstown Road, Port Melbourne, VIC 3207, Australia

314–321, 3rd Floor, Plot 3, Splendor Forum, Jasola District Centre, New Delhi – 110025, India

103 Penang Road, #05–06/07, Visioncrest Commercial, Singapore 238467

Cambridge University Press is part of Cambridge University Press & Assessment, a department of the University of Cambridge.

We share the University's mission to contribute to society through the pursuit of education, learning and research at the highest international levels of excellence.

www.cambridge.org
Information on this title: www.cambridge.org/9781009478526

DOI: 10.1017/9781009227223

First published 2024

A catalogue record for this publication is available from the British Library.

ISBN 978-1-009-47852-6 Hardback
ISBN 978-1-009-22726-1 Paperback
ISSN 2399-2883 (online)
ISSN 2514-3808 (print)

Iterative Conceptions of Set

Elements in the Philosophy of Mathematics

DOI: 10.1017/9781009227223
First published online: May 2024

Neil Barton
National University of Singapore and University of Oslo

Author for correspondence: Neil Barton, neilalexanderbarton@gmail.com

Abstract: Many philosophers are aware of the paradoxes of set theory (e.g. Russell's paradox). For many people, these were solved by the iterative conception of set which holds that sets are formed in stages by collecting sets available at previous stages. This Element will examine possibilities for articulating this solution. In particular, the author argues that there are different kinds of iterative conception, and it's open which of them (if any) is the best. Along the way, the intent of this Element is to make some of the underlying mathematical and philosophical ideas behind tricky bits of the philosophy of set theory clear for philosophers more widely and make their relationships to some other questions in philosophy perspicuous.

Keywords: set theory, iterative conception, uncountable sets, foundations of mathematics, infinity

ISBNs: 9781009478526 (HB), 9781009227261 (PB), 9781009227223 (OC)
ISSNs: 2399-2883 (online), 2514-3808 (print)

Contents

1 Introduction

If you're reading this Element, then I presume that you're curious about infinity, set theory, and its philosophy. Growing up, I'd always been interested in philosophy. Mathematics, however, I found to be a necessary but tiresome part of the curriculum, especially through my teenage years. I had great teachers, but the focus on exam preparation that inevitably took up the bulk of our time was just plain boring – solving dreary computational problems using known algorithmic methods (a task that I'm not especially good at to this day). This didn't fit so well with what my mother Jeanne (a mathematics teacher) had always told me – that at a certain point mathematical study can feel like 'doors opening left and right'. It was at university that I saw Cantor's theorem and Gödel's theorems for the first time. Suddenly I understood what my mum had meant – mathematics was an area where new ideas and methods could result in a complete shift in one's perspective on the world, and your ability to solve problems is only bounded by your creativity and the constraints of logical space. The doors were very much open, and I became increasingly interested in notions of infinity in mathematics. To understand infinity, it's very natural to start by considering our best mathematical theories of it. Set theory, as a theory of infinite collections and what we can do with them, was the obvious choice. Understandably, philosophers have shown a lot of interest in set theory since its beginnings in the late nineteenth and early twentieth centuries. There was already plenty of philosophical material to get my teeth into, and I tucked in with gusto.

What I discovered, however, was that the buffet was far richer than I had anticipated. In particular, several philosophical and mathematical advances have been made in the philosophy of set theory since the early 2000s. Both mathematicians and philosophers have closely examined ideas concerning whether there is an *all-encompassing domain* for set theory, and how the tools of contemporary set-theoretic practice might bear on philosophy. This has tied the study of the philosophy of set theory very closely to issues in *metaphysics*, including the nature of *possibility* and *absolute generality*. However, I think it's fair to say that these developments (with some notable exceptions) have been passed over for mainstream philosophical consideration. Whilst this is understandable – the mathematical barrier to entry is high and our time is finite – the philosophical issues themselves are (in my opinion) understandable to anyone with some introductory logic courses under their belt.

Many philosophers are aware of the *paradoxes* of set theory (e.g. Russell's paradox). Often people take these to be solved by the *iterative conception* of set which holds that sets are formed in stages by collecting together sets available at previous stages. This Element will examine possibilities for articulating this solution. In particular:

> **Main Aim** I will argue that there are different kinds of iterative conception, and it's open which of them (if any) is the best.

Along the way, I hope to make some of the underlying mathematical and philosophical ideas behind tricky bits of the philosophy of set theory clear for philosophers more widely, and make their relationship to other questions in philosophy perspicuous.

Here's the plan. Section 2 will lay down some reasons as to why we should be interested in set theory as philosophers and mathematicians. This section serves a dual purpose; first, as a motivation for the reader less familiar with set theory to get excited, and second, we'll see some desiderata that will be employed later in the Element when we come to assess set-theoretic conceptions.

Sections 3, 4, and 5 set up a way of thinking of set-theoretic progress as trading off inconsistent principles. Section 3 will go over the naive conception of set and the paradoxes that brought it down. We'll also provide a diagnosis of the problem as involving a conflict of two inconsistent principles. This material is well-worn, but I'll explain a twist on the classic paradoxes that has been examined by philosophers recently (namely that we can think of these paradoxes as being about the existence of *functions*) which will help integrate this material with what comes later. Section 4 will present the emergence of the *combinatorial conception* and *logical conception* of set, before Section 5 gives the *iterative conception* as a further sharpening of the combinatorial conception. We'll also explain the standard 'strong' version of the iterative conception and how it can be given a modal formulation.

Section 6 will then explain some mathematical ideas that have informed the development of contemporary set theory under the iterative conception, namely *forcing* (a way of adding subsets of sets to models). I'll do my best to make these mathematically tricky ideas palatable to philosophers.

Section 7 will explain two particular principles that we might take a very 'rich' conception of set to have and show them to be inconsistent. In particular, we'll see how the power-set axiom is incompatible with the idea that there should be saturation under forcing. We'll note that there's a similarity here with the situation we found ourselves in with respect to the naive conception, where a particular conception of set generates two inconsistent principles.

Sections 8 and 9 will identify a split in how we might move forward. Section 8 will explain how there is a genuine choice between powerset and forcing saturation, and will show how forcing saturation can be viewed as arising from kinds of set-construction method. Section 9 will explain how mathematics is interpreted within each conception and will contrast each in the light of the theoretical virtues discussed in Section 2.

Finally, Section 10 will provide a concluding summary and identify some further work that is needed in order to obtain greater clarity on these issues. In particular, I'll explain some salient objections that need addressing in order to move forward. I hope that the reader comes away with a sense of how set theory is philosophically interesting and the vastness of conceptual space.

Before we get going, however, a few remarks are in order. First, whilst I hope that this Element is of pedagogical value and can help people new to the philosophy of set theory gain an understanding of some difficult mathematics, *this is not a textbook*. My approach is one of conveying underlying ideas, rather than giving everything in full rigorous detail. Where sensible I've tried to give formal definitions and references for the interested reader in footnotes rather than the body of the text.

Relatedly, the pacing of this Element will feel slightly odd. There is a *tension in exposition* in that I both want to get the *newcomer* interested but also accomplish a significant *research-oriented* goal. I therefore run the risk of boring the reader who has been studying these issues for years whilst outstripping what can be expected of an early student (however talented). I've tried to present the known material in such a way that it makes recent novel twists on old material clear, and to keep the harder material as accessible as possible. However, this Element is *hard* if you aren't familiar with the relevant bits of mathematical logic. My aim is to make things *accessible* and not, per impossibile, *easy*. To combat this problem, the Element runs along two tracks. The 'standard' track is intended for those who do not necessarily have years of philosophy of set theory under their belt. The 'expert' track is for those who already know a good bit of philosophy of set theory. I denote sections/paragraphs/footnotes that are on the expert track with a 'blackbelt' emoji 🥋 (and often inside a box). I encourage everyone to read all the Element, after all it's helpful to peek behind the curtain and see some of the complicated workings of the machine. But readers should not feel disheartened if 🥋-parts are tricky to follow – those are especially difficult and one shouldn't expect to get everything on the first try.

I'll use the following conventions. Bits of language (e.g. syntax/utterances) will be enclosed within double quotation marks. So "Toffee is a clever cat" can be a sentence or an utterance, "cat" is a word or term of the English language, and "Toffee" is a name (in this context), whereas Toffee is a (particular) cat who is also clever. Single quotation marks will be used as 'scare quotes', namely cases where the enquoted phrase is not to be taken literally (though it may be illustrative). In cases where such usage occurs in a formal context, single quotes often denote an abbreviation for a formal claim (e.g. PA ⊢ 'There are infinitely many prime numbers', even though "There are infinitely many prime numbers" is a sentence of English, not Peano Arithmetic). Italics are reserved for emphasis, or where they occur in the scope of a definition, the definiendum. I allow definitions to be informal and philosophical as well as formal, but I will clearly separate the informal and formal definitions. With these conventions in hand, let's get ready to set out!

2 Why Set Theory?

Before we start getting into the iterative woods, I want to give some motivation for studying set theory and its philosophy.

Question Why do this, given that there are so many good introductions into these topics?

Answer As well as providing a survey of some of the literature, this section will lay down some *theoretical virtues* that we might think theories/conceptions of set can have. These virtues will be important later when we come to assessing our options.

What are sets? Here's a rough-and-ready definition:[1]

Definition 1 (Informal) A *set* is a kind of collection that is:

(i) **Extensional:** Sets with different members are non-identical, and sets with the same members are identical.
(ii) **Objectual:** Sets are *objects* over and above their elements.

So, for example, I can consider the set of books currently on my table. This is an object, in addition to the books themselves. If I take a book off my table, the term "the set of books on my table" now denotes a different set, since this new set of books has different members.

Just given this bare bones story, it's natural now to ask: **Why be interested in set theory at all?** It's useful first to consider a *bad* answer (but one that helps us see the *role* of set theory more clearly):

---

[1] ☜ It's plausible that nowadays we think that sets are *combinatorial* too (in the sense of being extensionally equivalent to pluralities of objects, irrespective of whether we can provide a circumscribing definition). Later we'll set up the difference between the logical conception and combinatorial conception of set, and so I don't want to commit to this just yet.

Theory of Collections Set theory provides our best theory of collections.

This is perhaps encapsulated by George Boolos' (1998) claim 'I thought that set theory was supposed to be a theory about all, 'absolutely' all, the collections that there were and that 'set' was synonymous with 'collection' (p. 35)[2]

The idea that the interest of set theory derives from 'set' being synonymous with 'collection' or providing our best theory of collections is open to at least two powerful criticisms. First, there are lots of different ways we talk about collections. To take two simple kinds: (1) Collection-like talk needn't be objectual. As the vast literature on plural logic indicates,[3] we can talk about and quantify over objects in the *plural* without thereby committing to a *set* of them. So, instead of talking about the *set* of books on my table, I could just have talked about *the books on my table* in the plural. (2) Collection-like talk needn't be extensional. Instead, it can be taken *intensionally*, where identity is not taken to be governed by an extensionality criterion. Presumably there's a sense in which I don't destroy my *beer coaster collection* just by giving one of the (many) beer coasters to a friend. My collection of beer coasters is just the kind of thing that can survive a loss (or better yet, gain) of some members.

Second, even if set theory did provide our best theory of collections, there's much more to the story. Collections of beer coasters are a perfectly good subject matter for philosophical study, but this observation fails to explain *why* set theory is often regarded as *central* to many areas (and especially mathematics).

Here's what I take to be the core point: *Objectual and extensional collections, when augmented with the 'right' axioms, are powerful devices of representation.* And the ability to *represent* means that all sorts of problems, both philosophical and mathematical, can be encoded within set theory.

Let's look at this idea in a little more detail. This representational power presents two interlinked aspects of set theory:

Foundation for Mathematics Set theory provides a 'foundation' for mathematics (and hence mathematical tools in philosophy).

Philosophical Repository Set theory examines many philosophically interesting subjects (e.g. paradoxes, infinity).

---

[2] Boolos here is discussing the contrast between sets and proper classes, so perhaps the quotation is intended for a slightly different context. Indeed, Boolos himself was key in the development and philosophical study of plural logic (see Boolos (1984) and so it's likely that he didn't think all collection-like talk had to be encapsulated by set theory. Whatever the weather, just putting the idea that set theory provides our best theory of collections out there is enough to get the ball rolling at this stage.

[3] See Florio and Linnebo (2021) for a book-length treatment.

This division is far from exclusive. Certainly there are cases where we might think that set theory and philosophy are inextricably intertwined.[4] Indeed, this Element emphasises the fact that mathematics and philosophy can become fruitfully intermixed, and I do not think it is either necessary or desirable to keep these considerations separate. Nor do I think that *every* bit of set theory will be entangled with philosophy, and there are set theorists who study solely mathematical questions. Still, the distinction serves as a rough categorisation for different facets of set theory.

At this stage, we'll keep things relatively informal, but a little precision will be helpful. One set theory that's proved to be of central interest is *Zermelo–Fraenkel set theory with the Axiom of Choice* (ZFC), which we'll examine more closely later. For now let's just content ourselves with the following rough characterisation: ZFC tells you that there are lots of sets (both finite and infinite) and lets you do many of the usual set-theoretic operations you want on those sets (e.g. take the union of two sets).

Recently, Penelope Maddy has isolated some *mathematical goals* of set-theoretic foundations built on ZFC.[5] I'll provide some examination of Maddy's ideas, and I'll suggest some modifications and additions of my own.[6] These goals serve a dual purpose. On the one hand, they motivate the consideration of set theory for the interested reader. On the other, we will use them later to evaluate particular conceptions of set.

Earlier I mentioned that set theory is a powerful device of *representation*. Many of the desiderata we'll consider are linked to this idea. For instance:

Observation We can encode/represent all mathematical objects using sets.[7]

What do I mean by 'encode/represent' here? Let's take a simple example from high-school mathematics. We want to consider some geometric object in two-dimensional (Euclidean) space, let's say a straight line. By picking an origin and imposing a coordinate system, we can represent this straight line by some function $f(x) = bx + c$ and think of the straight line as composed of its

---

[4] See, for example, Rittberg (2020) who argues that set-theoretic mathematical practice can be metaphysically laden.

[5] See Maddy (2017) and Maddy (2019).

[6] For clarity's sake, **Generous Arena**, **Shared Standard**, **Metamathematical Corral**, and **Risk Assessment** are all explicitly identified by Maddy, and **Theory of Collections**, **Foundation for Mathematics**, **Philosophical Repository**, **Theory of Infinity**, **Independence**, **Limits of Formalisation**, and **Testing Ground for Paradox** are my own additions (though many are implicit in much of the literature and Maddy's work).

[7] See Posy (2020), section 2, for a very concise survey of the classical situation (Posy sets up the classical mathematician as a foil for intuitionism), as well as many set theory textbooks (e.g. Enderton (1977).

graph of ordered pairs $\langle x, bx + c \rangle$. This can help us when, for example, trying to compute the relative lengths of line segments (e.g. by using the Pythagorean theorem). But the ordered pairs aren't (intuitively speaking) *the same* as the line, they just *encode* it.

So with sets, but generalised to any mathematical object you'd care to consider. Zero can be encoded by the empty set, natural numbers by the finite von Neumann ordinals,[8] rationals as pairs of natural numbers, reals as Dedekind cuts of rationals,[9] ordered pairs as Kuratowski ordered pairs,[10] and functions/relations by sets of ordered pairs (i.e. the function f is encoded by $\{\langle x,y \rangle | f(x) = y\}$). Of course, there are lots of choices, and this is just an illustration of *one* way you might do things.[11]

Using similar tactics, any mathematical object we have come up with can be encoded by sets (putting aside some controversial cases).[12] This has some important consequences. First, set theory provides a:

Generous Arena Find *representatives* for our usual mathematical structures (e.g. $\mathbb{N}$, $\mathbb{R}$) using our theory of sets.

I think it is worth pausing for a moment to reflect on just how remarkable **Generous Arena** is. Just using the membership relation and suitable axioms, we can find a representative for almost any object you'd care to discuss – all the vertiginous diversity we see in mathematics can be captured by that one little relation of membership.[13] Because we can encode mathematical objects as sets, we have a way of relating them to each other within a single domain. This, Maddy argues, gives us:

Shared Standard Provide a standard of correctness for proof in mathematics.

---

[8] These can be defined inductively with $0 =_{df} \emptyset$ and $n + 1 =_{df} n \cup \{n\}$.

[9] A Dedekind cut is a partition of the rational numbers into two non-empty sets A and B, where A is closed downwards and does not contain a greatest element.

[10] The *Kuratowski ordered pair* is given by $\langle a, b \rangle =_{df} \{\{a\}, \{a, b\}\}$.

[11] See Barton et al. (2022) for some of the formal details and further citations.

[12] For example, one controversial objection (e.g. Mac Lane (1986) and Muller (2001)) to set theory goes something like this: 'Everything in set theory has to be encoded by a set, and we know that some categories like the category of all sets are too big to be encoded by sets. So set theory cannot provide a foundation for category theory.' I do not find this objection convincing for the following two reasons. (1) set theorists certainly *seem* to talk about proper-class-sized objects – the study of proper classes is in my (controversial) opinion a perfectly legitimate part of set theory, and (2) I don't think that category-theoretic study of the sets is really directed at the study of *all the sets*, but rather the study of the schematic first-order properties that all the sets happen to satisfy. A full defence of this idea will have to be left for a different day, but a more detailed explanation of this point can be found in Barton and Friedman (2019) (esp. section 10.3).

[13] We'll see how this formally plays out when we come to talk about the language of set theory – see Definition 12 in Section 3.2.

The thought here is that because we have **Generous Arena** and can view mathematical objects as encoded/represented by sets, a proof about a mathematical object can be regarded as correct if it could be (in principle) translated into a proof in set theory about properties of the relevant mathematical code(s). Of course, 'in principle' is *important* here – outside of set-theoretic mathematics it is very clunky to work with these codes, and we shouldn't expect mathematicians to actually go about their daily lives solely using the language of set theory. The relevant language of the discipline in question is probably more flexible than working with just membership. (A desire for a foundation that 'will capture the fundamental character of mathematics as it's actually done, that will guide mathematicians toward the truly important concepts and structures, without getting bogged down in irrelevant details' Maddy terms **Essential Guidance**, and since all set theories we'll consider here perform pretty badly in this respect, we'll set it to one side.)[14]

The ability to manipulate large infinite collections in ZFC-based set theory yields the following:

Theory of Infinity Set theory provides our best theory of infinite numbers.

Theory of Infinity will be important later and so I've explicitly identified it as a theoretical virtue in contrast to some of the literature that leaves it implicit (it does not occur, for example, amongst the virtues identified by Maddy (2017) and Maddy (2019)). To see its significance, we start by examining the two main kinds of infinite number in set theory, namely *ordinal* and *cardinal* numbers. An *ordinal* number can be thought of as an answer to the question of how *long* an infinite ordering is. Call a set x (under a linear relation R) *well-ordered by R* if and only if every subset of x has an R-least element. If x is well-ordered by R, then there's no way of descending infinitely in x along R. This helps us think of performing *actions* or *operations* into the infinite along a suitable infinite relation. Within ZFC one can represent and develop an arithmetic for these orders, defining notions of *ordinal addition, multiplication*, and *exponentiation*.[15] This provides us with ways of generalising normally finite operations (e.g. computation) into the infinite.[16]

---

[14] See Maddy (2017), p. 305.

[15] There are lots of ways to do this, but one popular way is to use von Neumann ordinals, where we let $0 = \emptyset$, $\alpha + 1 = \alpha \cup \{\alpha\}$, and limit $\lambda = \bigcup_{\beta < \lambda} \beta$. Addition is represented by the *ordered disjoint union*, multiplication by the *lexicographical ordering* on the *product*, and exponentiation by *iterated multiplication*.

[16] For example, we can consider *infinite time* Turing machines. See Hamkins and Lewis (2000).

Cardinal numbers, by contrast, can be thought of as answers to the question of how *many* objects there are in a set. In particular, we say that two sets X and Y *have the same cardinality* if and only if there is a bijection between them, where a *bijection* $f\colon X \rightarrowtail\!\!\!\!\rightarrow Y$ is a function that 'pairs off' the members of X and Y, that is, f takes no two elements of X to the same element of Y (f is *injective*) and every element of Y is hit by f applied to some element of X (f is *surjective*). By representing cardinals using particular kinds of sets, ZFC provides a theory in which the cardinal sizes of any sets can be compared and natural operations like multiplication, addition, and exponentiation generalised and computed.[17] The success of ZFC is striking; it seemingly gives finite beings (e.g. us) the ability to reason about large infinite objects. Many surprising facts can be thereby shown. For example, we can prove:

Theorem 2 *There are as many natural numbers as there are squares of natural numbers (in particular $f(x) = x^2$ is just such a bijection from the natural numbers to the squares of naturals).*

This is somewhat surprising since the squares of n and $n + 1$ get more and more spread out as n gets larger. Indeed, similar results were even regarded as kinds of 'paradox' by Thābit ibn Qurra and Galileo. We can even show:

Theorem 3 *The set of all* rational numbers – *the numbers expressible by fractions* – *is the same size as the set of all natural numbers.*[18]

This is so even though there are infinitely many rational numbers between any two natural numbers. We can also show:

Theorem 4 *There are as many real numbers between* 0 *and* 1 *(or any two real numbers for that matter) as there are in the real line, or in any n-dimensional plane based on the real line (i.e.* $\mathbb{R}^n$*).*[19]

Despite these surprising results on *sameness of size*, we also discovered that infinity comes in *different* cardinal sizes:

Theorem 5 (*Cantor's theorem for the reals*) *The cardinality of real numbers is greater in size than the cardinality of the natural numbers, in the sense that*

---

[17] Again, there's a variety of ways one might proceed, but here's a typical one. The *cardinality of X* can be represented as the least von Neumann ordinal bijective with X. Cardinal addition can be computed as the cardinality of the disjoint union, multiplication as the cardinality of the product, and exponentiation X^Y as the cardinality of the set of all functions from Y to X.

[18] See, for example, chapter 2 of Giaquinto (2002) for an explanation of this result.

[19] Again, see chapter 2 of Giaquinto (2002).

(i) there is no bijection between the natural numbers and the real numbers, and
(ii) there is an injection from the natural numbers to the real numbers.

This phenomenon appears to be more general than merely comparing the natural numbers and real numbers. We in fact discovered that:

Theorem 6 (*Cantor's theorem*) *Let* $\mathcal{P}(x)$ *denote the powerset of x, the set of all subsets of x (that such a set always exists is one of the central axioms of ZFC). Then the cardinality of* $\mathcal{P}(x)$ *is greater than that of x.*[20]

Again, Cantor's theorem is striking. It seems to imply, on the basis of natural principles about sets, that if there's one infinite set, then there's a *never-ending hierarchy* of infinite sets, since the powerset of any set x is always bigger than x. Moreover, it produces much of the interest of cardinal arithmetic – whilst addition and multiplication are trivial for infinite cardinal numbers (one can show that both addition and multiplication just result in getting the larger of the two back), cardinal exponentiation is *not* – one can show that $2^\kappa > \kappa$ for any cardinal κ.[21]

The ability to work with infinity plays out in various areas of philosophy, including areas outside the philosophy of mathematics.[22] Indeed, these arguments are often regarded as a refutation of the time-honoured position in philosophy and mathematics that infinity is completely beyond understanding and intractable.[23]

---

[20] We'll discuss a proof of Cantor's theorem later, in particular as it relates to the paradoxes in Section 3.

[21] In particular, you can think of 2^κ as the size of $\mathcal{P}(\kappa)$, since any member of $\mathcal{P}(\kappa)$ can be correlated with a unique function from κ to $2 = \{0, 1\}$ via *characteristic functions* (where for $X \subseteq \kappa, f(\alpha) = 1$ if and only if $\alpha \in X$).

[22] Here's an example from infinite ethics showing how infinite assumptions can play out with utility calculations (the example is due to Cain (1995). Suppose we have people arranged at all coordinates of the real plane indexed by integers (so there's a single person at every (m, n) for integers m and n). A circle slowly grows from the origin. In one scenario (the *circle of happiness*), everyone starts at utility -1 and moves to utility $+1000$ (or any large finite amount) when they fall inside the perimeter of the circle (and remains at this value forevermore). For the *circle of negativity*, each agent starts at $+1$ and goes to -1000 when they get caught by the circle. With simple cardinality arguments one can argue that the sum of the utility for the expanding sphere of negativity is positively infinite, whereas the expanding sphere of happiness is negatively infinite (one needs to define these terms, but the rough idea is that there's always boundedly many happy/sad people in the circle of happiness/negativity, whereas infinitely many people of the opposite disposition). Cain argues that we should nonetheless *prefer* to be in the expanding happiness world (since then we just have to wait long enough to be blissfully happy forevermore). Thanks to Joel David Hamkins for communicating this example to me; see Hamkins and Montero (2000) for some further discussion.

[23] See, for example, the paradoxes of the infinite given in the Introduction to Moore (1990). The place of Cantor, his results, and other scholars in arriving at a final acceptance of infinity is actually somewhat more subtle than is often acknowledged (see Ferreirós (2007), especially

However, this success must be tempered by the following phenomenon that emerged in the twentieth century:

Independence There are sentences of set theory that can neither be proved nor refuted using our 'canonical' theory of sets ZFC, assuming that ZFC is consistent. Nor can any 'reasonable' expansion of ZFC settle all questions formalisable in the language of set theory.[24]

Before we discuss this further, let's remark that the *mere fact* of independence is philosophically important. It shows that there will be limits to what any single formal theory can capture. There are at least two kinds of independence that will be relevant for us. To set things up, let's start with the following:

Definition 7 We let the cardinal numbers be indexed by ordinals using a function we'll call the 'aleph' function (or $\aleph$). $\aleph_0$ is the smallest cardinal number (which happens to be the cardinality of the natural numbers). $\aleph_1$ is the next smallest, and more generally $\aleph_\alpha$ is the αth cardinal number. We'll denote the ordinal corresponding to $\aleph_\alpha$ by ω_α (we'll often also let ω_0 be denoted by "ω").

A routine argument shows that $2^{\aleph_0} > \aleph_0$ (by Cantor's theorem). But is there anything in between? That is, does $2^{\aleph_0} = \aleph_1$? Or are there intermediate cardinalities, and in fact $2^{\aleph_0} > \aleph_1$?

Definition 8 We will use the following for discussing the spread of cardinalities:

- The *Continuum Hypothesis* (or CH) is the statement that $2^{\aleph_0} = \aleph_1$.
- The *Generalised Continuum Hypothesis* (or GCH) is the statement that 'For every ordinal α, $2^{\aleph_\alpha} = \aleph_{\alpha+1}$' (i.e. every jump in cardinality obtained by applying the powerset operation to an infinite set just pushes you up *one* cardinal number).
- The *continuum function* is defined by $f(\aleph_\alpha) = 2^{\aleph_\alpha}$ (i.e. the function that takes an infinite cardinal to the cardinality of its powerset).

---

the Introduction). In particular, it is somewhat unclear whether our notion of cardinality *had* to be the Cantorian one, or we might have ended up with a version of cardinality that respects the idea that a proper part should always be smaller than the whole. Paolo Mancosu has championed this idea; see Mancosu (2009) for analysis and references to its mathematical development (e.g. in the work of Katz, Benci, Di Nasso, and Forti). Gödel provides an argument that the right notion of cardinality is Cantorian in the opening to his paper on the continuum hypothesis (Gödel (1947), with revisions in Gödel (1964)), which has in turn been critically examined by Matthew Parker (see Parker (2019)).

[24] Here 'reasonable' means recursively enumerable and consistent.

As it turns out, CH, ¬CH, GCH, and ¬GCH are all consistent with ZFC (assuming ZFC itself is consistent). We'll explain how this works later (Section 6).

To discuss the other kind of independence, we first need a brief foray into *consistency strengths*. Within arithmetic, and hence within ZFC, one can (computably) encode syntactic notions like *sentence, formula, proof,* and *consistency*. This allows you to formulate a sentence within ZFC expressing the idea that ZFC is itself consistent (more precisely, you can formalise within ZFC the sentence that there's no proof of a contradiction derivable from the axioms of ZFC). Call this sentence *Con*(ZFC). But now we can point to:

Theorem 9 (Gödel's second incompleteness theorem) *Assuming that* ZFC *is consistent, then neither Con*(ZFC) *nor ¬Con*(ZFC) *is provable in* ZFC. *Moreover, this theorem holds for any (suitably nice)[25] theory that can represent arithmetic.*

Within set theory we can study a wide variety of sentences that have different consistency strengths – one can often prove one extension of ZFC consistent from another. As it turns out, CH and ¬CH are *not* like this (ZFC, ZFC + CH, and ZFC + ¬CH are all *equiconsistent* in that one can prove each consistent from the other). Obviously adding *Con*(ZFC) results in a consistency strength increase. There are other principles – so-called *large cardinal axioms* – that are important here. These serve as the natural indices for consistency strength. They postulate the existence of sets with a lot of *closure* properties and if they exist (or are consistent) we can prove that many theories are consistent by finding *models* of the relevant kind. Set theory has in fact discovered a whole hierarchy of these cardinals with stronger and stronger closure properties.

🕸 Here's an example:

Definition 10 A cardinal κ is *strongly inaccessible* (or just *inaccessible*) if and only if:

  (i) κ is uncountable (i.e. it's bigger than the cardinality of natural numbers).
  (ii) Given any set x smaller than κ, the cardinality of $\mathcal{P}(x)$ is also smaller than κ. Such κ are called *strong limit cardinals*.

---

[25] 🕸 Namely recursively enumerable and consistent.

(iii) Given any set x smaller than κ, and any function $f: x \to \kappa$, the range of f is bounded by some $\gamma < \kappa$. That is, given such an x and $f: x \to \kappa$, we always have some $\gamma < \kappa$ such that for every $y \in x$, $f(y) < \gamma$. Here, we say that κ is *regular*.

It's instructive to think about what such an axiom says. Such a κ seems very big – clause (i) ensures it's bigger than $\mathbb{N}$, (ii) says that you can't catch it with something smaller by taking our favourite size-increasing operation (powerset), and clause (iii) says that you can't catch it by mapping a smaller object into it using a function. One can show that an inaccessible cardinal κ suffices to produce a model for ZFC (and much more), and so by Gödel's second incompleteness theorem you can't produce an inaccessible cardinal from ZFC alone. We can strengthen this axiom by postulating that there is a cardinal κ that is (i) strongly inaccessible, and (ii) has κ-many strongly inaccessibles beneath it. And these cardinals lie *right at the bottom* of the large cardinal hierarchy.[a]

---

[a] See, for example, the diagram on p. 472 of Kanamori (2009) for an idea of the extent of the space.

Those are the two kinds of independence we'll consider. One (the CH kind), results in no increase in consistency strength and often involves the relative sizes of infinite cardinals. The other (the large cardinal kind) involves increases in consistency strength, and one way to calibrate this is by considering sets with ever greater and greater closure properties. These aren't the only kinds of independence (there are also strong axioms that don't directly postulate the existence of large cardinals)[26] but these are the ones we'll focus on.

We should pause for a moment to reflect on what this independence tells us about our ability to provide formalisations of theories of sets. Whilst ZFC does give us the resources to prove a great many things about the infinite, it does not yield information about the values of many cardinal computations nor what kinds of set exist with certain closure properties. How we might respond to this situation will be a central theme of this Element, but it should be noted that **Independence** is a reason for philosophers – that is, not just mathematicians – to be interested in set theory. Assessing the impact of independence is central for understanding how our thought, language, and theories relate to the world and what we can (and maybe can't) do. I think it's important therefore to isolate the following philosophical aspect of set theory.

---

[26] See, for example, so-called Axioms of Definable Determinacy (Koellner, 2014).

Limits of Formalisation Set theory provides a natural place to examine the limits of our formalisation, pushing the boundaries of what might be realistically expected to be captured, and exploring where formalisations may finally give out.

It's a beguiling question to think what the implications of **Limits of Formalisation** might be. Does it imply that there are limits on what can be known? Or that there is some kind of metaphysical indeterminacy in the world? These are important questions for philosophers, and show that **Independence** is not merely a mathematical curio.

From the mathematical perspective, set theory is one of the main theories in which we study **Independence**. It provides us with flexible tools with which we can study models of different theories, how they can be built from one another, and hence how relative provability works (given the completeness theorem). We can thus (with Maddy) identify:

Metamathematical Corral Provide a theory in which metamathematical investigations of relative provability and consistency strengths can be easily conducted.[27]

As philosophers, we should be keen to assess whether the theories we work in are consistent. **Metamathematical Corral** combined with the fact (as we'll see later) that set theory often comes with an attendant conception of what the sets are like gives us:

Risk Assessment Provide a degree of confidence in theories commensurate with their consistency strength.

In particular, suppose that you come up with a wild new theory T (either philosophical or mathematical). If I can use some set theory S to produce a model of T, then I know that I can be at least as confident in the consistency of T as I am in S.

Risk Assessment is especially important, as many theories here are *inconsistent*. As many philosophers know, early set theory was subject to paradoxes

---

[27] $\frac{1}{\pi}$ As experts will know, there are other theories we might pick. One only really *needs* a theory of syntax to study consistency (and weak theories of arithmetic suffice for such a theory). Another salient field here is proof theory and the study of proof-theoretic ordinals. In a way, set theory provides *more* than what is required for examining **Metamathematical Corral**. However, it is in the variety of *models*, and what one can build from them, where set theory really shines. So it is perhaps better to say that set theory provides a piece of the puzzle for **Metamathematical Corral**, rather than the whole picture. Thanks to Marcus Giaquinto and Daniel Waxman for some further discussion here.

(e.g. Russell's Paradox). However set theory can also yield inconsistency and paradox when combined with other philosophical principles, such as when we layer mereology on top of the sets (e.g. Uzquiano (2006)). I also want to point out (in line with **Philosophical Repository**) that an *enormous* variety of set-theoretic ideas can be extended to inconsistency. In particular when we push ideas to their natural limit, they nearly always explode. Perhaps this constitutes a kind of 'paradox' (maybe in a weak sense of the term). Some of these we'll see later, and some others I mention in a footnote for the reader who wants to look further.[28] One might think that this is a negative of the discipline – after all, isn't inconsistency an (if not *the*) unforgivable sin? I disagree. Inconsistency can be informative. Set theory gives us the tools to locate and diagnose these inconsistencies, helping us to elucidate our **Limits of Formalisation** and further giving us a:

Testing Ground for Paradox Set theory is very *paradox* prone, both in terms of the principles that can be formulated within set theory and when combined with certain philosophical ideas (e.g. absolute generality and mereology). In this way, set theory provides a *testing ground* for seeing when and how ideas are inconsistent.

So, there's some interesting and nice features of set theory – not just a **Theory of Collections**, but a field that provides a **Foundation for Mathematics** and **Philosophical Repository**, in particular by yielding a **Generous Arena**, **Shared Standard, Theory of Infinity**, the example of **Independence** and its use as a **Testing Ground for Paradox**, that help articulate the **Limits of Formalisation**, give us a **Metamathematical Corral**, and **Risk Assessment** for our theories. Before we move on, I want to identify one last important aspect of set theory. Although many of the preceding constraints are simply reasons to be interested in set theory, or are things that set theory has happened to be useful for, there is a sense in which set theory was *designed* to fit these purposes. **Risk Assessment**, for example, can't go ahead without set theorists *deliberately* studying **Independence** and **Metamathematical Corral**. In this way, many of the preceding features – notably **Generous Arena, Shared Standard, Theory of Infinity, Metamathematical Corral,** and **Risk Assessment** – are not just pleasant features of set theory, but constraints/desiderata on its development

---

28   For example, the embedding template $j \colon V \to M$ for large cardinals explodes when $M = V$. Forcing axioms can pop in various ways, either by admitting too many parameters, allowing too many kinds of forcing, or not keeping a tight enough control on the sentences allowed (see Bagaria (2005)). Standard reflection principles blow up at the level of third-order reflection (see Reinhardt (1974) and Koellner (2009)) and modal reflection principles are pretty flammable too (see Roberts (2019)).

too. Indeed this is one of the central points of Maddy (2017) and Maddy (2019), (though she leaves **Theory of Infinity** implicit). Thinking about these virtues in this dual light will help to illuminate some of the issues later, and in particular whether different conceptions/theories of sets are *virtuous*. We'll see some more virtues in due course, and for ease they are collated in Section 9.3.

3 The Naive Conception of Set and the Classic Paradoxes

We've now got some virtues of set theory on the table (Section 2). In this section I want to explain one role for conceptions of set (namely to motivate theories) and revisit some well-known material on the naive conception of set and the 'classic' set-theoretic paradoxes. In doing so, I'll present a way of looking at the paradoxes in terms of *functions*.

3.1 Conceptions of Set and Motivating Theories

One way into the problem of the paradoxes is by considering the following:

Question What do we *want* out of a conception of set?

At least in this partly philosophical and partly mathematical context, what we want out of a conception is a *satisfying motivation* for a *good theory*, and this is what I'll take the primary purpose of a conception of set to be in this Element. Let's now clarify these notions a little.

Regarding the theory motivated: What we really want is a theory that can be made suitably *precise*. For this, I'll assume that we want to motivate an *axiomatic theory*.[29] I'll presuppose that the reader has some understanding of formal axiomatic theories (later we'll use a little bit of first-order predicate logic, plural logic, modal logic, and set theory). Where possible, I'll provide informal paraphrases and reference away the formal details.

Regarding the notions of a *good theory* and a *satisfying motivation*: We've seen some constraints on a good theory in Section 2. For example, a good theory should provide a **Generous Arena** and enable **Metamathematical Corral**. As we proceed, we'll discuss the virtues from Section 2 in more detail with respect to specific proposals for the theories we adopt. Motivations, on the other hand, might take the form of a formalisation (as we'll see later with various *modal set theories*), but equally they could be something more informal. In particular, we'll talk of *conceptions* of set. These can be thought of as informal descriptions of what the sets are like, which might then be formalised in various ways.

---

[29] Here I am following some of the remarks in ch. 1 of Incurvati (2020).

There's a lot to say about the nature of conceptions, but we'll avoid getting into these tricky issues here (though we will mention some open questions in Section 10).[30]

Whether these *motivations* on the basis of *conceptions* are *satisfying* also presents a rather tricky cluster of problems. But some progress can be made again by thinking about the goals from Section 2 and examining how the theories proposed enable set theory to fulfil its usual roles. But we'll also be able to isolate some further desiderata on conceptions of set as we proceed, aside from Section 2's virtues pertaining to set theory more broadly. This latter target we'll accomplish in Sections 4 and 5.

3.2 The Naive Conception of Set

Our first conception will be the naive conception of set:

Definition 11 (Informal) The *naive conception* of set holds that sets are extensions of predicates, where the extension of a predicate is the collection of all the things to which the predicate applies.[31]

We now want to consider what axioms the naive conception motivates. For this, it will be helpful to set up an important language for us:

Definition 12 The *language of set theory* or $\mathscr{L}_\in$ is the first-order language with one non-logical binary predicate "$\in$" and well-formed formulas formed in the obvious way. (**Note:** We include identity as part of first-order logic throughout this Element.)

The naive conception clearly motivates adoption of the *extensionality axiom* (which says that any two sets with the same members are equal) as it is a conception of set. Unfortunately, it also motivates:

Definition 13 The *Naive Comprehension Schema* asserts that for every one-place formula $\phi(x)$ in the language of set theory $\mathscr{L}_\in$, there is a set of all and only the sets satisfying $\phi(x)$. Formally:

$$(\exists y)(\forall z)(z \in y \leftrightarrow \phi(z))$$

Sadly, as we know, the Naive Comprehension Schema is inconsistent. Let's see how.

---

[30] See Incurvati (2020, p. 13) for discussion.
[31] This formulation is taken directly from Incurvati (2020, p. 24).

3.3 The Paradoxes

Why go over the paradoxes, when excellent introductions are available in a wide variety of texts?[32] Aren't we just rehashing old material? Here's why we'll look at them:

(1) Part of what we will see later is a 'new' kind of paradox (the Cohen–Scott Paradox) and we'll discuss how it's similar to the classic paradoxes. So getting them on the table early is a good idea.

(2) There has been a shift of focus in the philosophical literature towards viewing the paradoxes as concerned with the (non-)existence of particular *functions*. Aside from the fact that these presentations are independently interesting, this way of viewing the paradoxes will help us see the afore-mentioned similarities a little better.

In this Element, I'll only really consider Russell's Paradox and Cantor's Paradox. The Burali–Forti Paradox is also interesting; however, it is complicated by the fact that one has to use set-theoretic codes for the ordinals (which otherwise could be thought of as sui generis mathematical objects).[33] Here they are:

Russell's Paradox Consider the condition $x \notin x$. By Naive Comprehension, this determines a set r. We ask: "Is $r \in r$?" If yes, then $r \notin r$ (since r is in the set of all $x \notin x$), contradiction. So, instead assume $r \notin r$. Then r satisfies the condition $x \notin x$, and so $r \in r$, contradiction. But then $r \in r \leftrightarrow r \notin r$, a contradiction!

Cantor's Paradox Consider the condition $x = x$. Let $\{x | x = x\}$ be denoted by u (for "universal set"). Now consider $\mathcal{P}(u)$, namely the *powerset* of u. By Naive Comprehension, this is also a set. Now we show $x = \mathcal{P}(u)$ by noting: (i) every element of $\mathcal{P}(u)$ is an element of u (trivially), and (ii) if $x \in u$, then $x \in \mathcal{P}(u)$ (since if $x \in u$, then $\forall y \in x, y \in u$ (i.e. $x \subseteq u$) and so $x \in \mathcal{P}(u)$). So, $u = \mathcal{P}(u)$.

Clearly then, there is a surjection[a] $f: u \twoheadrightarrow \mathcal{P}(u)$. Now consider the set $c = \{x | x \notin f(x)\}$. Since f is surjective, there is a $y \in u$ such that $f(y) = c$. We now ask "Is $y \in c$?" If yes (i.e. $y \in c$), then $y \in f(y)$, but then y violates c's defining condition, and so $y \notin c$, contradiction. So then we assume

---

[32] See, for example, Giaquinto (2002), Potter (2004), and Incurvati (2020), for philosophical introductions to the paradoxes, but almost any introductory text on set theory will cover them.

[33] For some discussion of these issues, see Menzel (1986), Shapiro and Wright (2006), Menzel (2014), and Florio and Leach-Krouse (2017).

$y \notin c$. But then $y \notin f(y)$, and so y meets c's defining condition, and $y \in c$, contradiction. So $y \in c \leftrightarrow y \notin c$, a contradiction!

In fact, this proof can be transformed into a proof of Cantor's *theorem*, just by replacing u by any old set x and performing a reductio on the claim that there is a surjection $f: x \twoheadrightarrow \mathcal{P}(x)$.

---

[a] As a reminder: A *surjection* $f: x \twoheadrightarrow y$ is a function such that for every $y_1 \in y$, there is an $x_1 \in x$ such that $f(x_1) = y_1$ (i.e. every member of y gets hit by f applied to some element of x).

So far, so well-known. Many introductory textbooks contain a presentation of the paradoxes. However, something philosophers have paid more attention to recently (though it has been known for a long time) is that these paradoxes are *closely related*:[34]

The Cantor–Russell Paradox Define u and $\mathcal{P}(u)$ as in Cantor's Paradox. Consider the case where our surjection $f: u \twoheadrightarrow \mathcal{P}(u)$ is the *identity map* $f(x) = x$. Now the problematic set $c = \{y | y \notin f(y)\} = \{y | y \notin y\} = r$. We'll also refer to this a the Cantor–Russell reasoning.

The important thing to note is that in this context (where f is the identity map) the contradictory set r we get out is the problematic set for *both* the Cantor and Russell reasoning (since f is the identity map here, the set $\{y | y \notin f(y)\}$ *just is* $\{y | y \notin y\}$). So the two are not just *superficially* similar, but in many contexts come down to definition of *exactly the same set*, and the core issue is whether there's a surjection $f: u \twoheadrightarrow \mathcal{P}(u)$.

This observation works in the other direction too, where we assume that we have an *injection*[35] $f: \mathcal{P}(u) \rightarrowtail u$. Without loss of generality, again this can be the identity map (since $\mathcal{P}(u) = u$). Now we can just consider the set $\{y | y \notin f^{-1}(y)\}$ (this is well defined since f is an injection).

Cantor's Paradox and Russell's Paradox might still not be *exactly* the same (Cantor's Paradox uses a bit more machinery than Russell's, e.g. injections), but there are clearly strong similarities between the two. I'll remain neutral on whether they are really 'the same' in any deep sense. Important for later will just be:

(1) We can view each paradox as starting by postulating the existence of a particular kind of function (either a surjection or an injection).

---

[34] See, in particular, Bell (2014), Whittle (2015), Meadows (2015), Whittle (2018), Incurvati (2020), Scambler (2021), and Builes and Wilson (2022).

[35] Another reminder: An *injection* $f: x \rightarrowtail y$ is a function such that for $x_1, x_2 \in x$, if $f(x_1) = f(x_2)$, then $x_1 = x_2$ (i.e. f doesn't take any two distinct elements of x to the same thing in y).

(2) We can then identify sets x and y such that $x \in y \leftrightarrow x \notin y$ (in the case of Cantor–Russell, x and y are both r).[36]

3.4 Universality and Indefinite Extensibility

So, Naive Comprehension leads to contradiction. But *why*, and what *options* are we left with? Many have been considered throughout the literature, surveys are available in Giaquinto (2002), Priest (2002), and Incurvati (2020). We'll follow Incurvati's presentation here, since it will be instructive for making comparisons.

Let's start by noting that the Naive Comprehension Schema encodes the following principle about the concept of set:

Universality A concept/conception C is universal if and only if there exists a set of all the things falling under C.[37]

Universality clearly follows from the naive conception, since the condition $x = x$ is a perfectly legitimate predicate of set theory and the naive conception immediately licences the Naive Comprehension Schema. However, the following is also a consequence:

Indefinite extensibility A concept/conception C is indefinitely extensible if and only if whenever we succeed in defining a set u of objects falling under C, there is an operation which, given u, produces an object falling under C but not belonging to u.[38]

Indefinite extensibility also follows from the Naive Comprehension Schema. This is because any time we have a set x, the Naive Comprehension Schema gives us the juice required for the Cantor–Russell reasoning, and we can then diagonalise to find a set not in x (e.g. one of the members of $\mathcal{P}(x)$).[39]

Clearly, any conception that validates both **Universality** and **Indefinite Extensibility** will be inconsistent, since there both must and can't be a set of all objects falling under the conception. So in order to proceed, a natural way to go is to examine conceptions of set that drop one of these fundamental principles.

---

[36] Of course, strictly speaking, anything follows from the contradiction in classical logic. The point is just that a natural way of reasoning to the contradiction is to note the contradictory membership conditions.

[37] This is adapted from Incurvati (2020), p. 27.

[38] Again, adapted from Incurvati (2020), p. 27.

[39] This way of looking at things has clear affinities with Priest's (2002) characterisation of the Inclosure Schema and Domain Principle. Since we're concentrating on set theory here, and Priest's framework is more general, I've chosen to go the Incurvati route.

And this is just what iterative set theories do. First though, we'll look at a more coarse-grained distinction between the *logical* and *combinatorial* conceptions of set.

4 The Logical and Combinatorial Conceptions of Set

We found ourselves in a tricky situation at the turn of the twentieth century. The burgeoning field of set theory was clearly *useful*, but the naive conception of set was *deeply* flawed. How to respond to this state of affairs?

In this section I want to make a preliminary distinction between the *logical* and *combinatorial* conceptions of set. This distinction will be pretty rough-and-ready, but it will help to elucidate the strategy for the rest of the Element when we come to discuss iterative conceptions. Before we get going, I want to lay down some further desiderata on conceptions of set, to complement the broader goals of set theory presented in Section 2. These will help us in comparing different conceptions moving forward.

4.1 Further Desiderata on Conceptions of Set

Earlier, we remarked that we want a conception of set to *motivate* a *good* theory of sets, and do so in a *satisfying* way. It's now time to elucidate a little more what we'd like out of these notions.

For starters, it's desirable for a conception to have the following feature:

Naturalness Provide a reasonably natural account of what the sets are like, one which avoids ad hoc restrictions.

For example, if I tweak the naive conception of set to say that wherever an instance would lead to inconsistency it should be rejected, I have made a purely ad hoc restriction that is not clearly motivated by the underlying conception. According to the desideratum of **Naturalness**, we should avoid these kinds of move – the needed restrictions should flow naturally from the underlying informal idea provided.[40]

We want more than merely the underlying picture to be natural though; we should want it to motivate a good theory of sets (where 'good', as discussed in Section 2, is likely to need some spelling out). So, we identify:

---

[40] Though see Goldstein (2012) for a view that tries to advocate this position. The view has roots at least far back as Quine, and something like it may even have been held by Zermelo (see Maddy (1988a)). There are also mathematical difficulties in actually carrying out this project due to the existence of mutually incompatible maximally consistent sets of instances of naive comprehension. See Incurvati and Murzi (2017).

Interpretation A conception should motivate a good theory of sets.

Given the background of classical logic, inconsistent theories of sets are *trivial* (everything follows by the principle of explosion). In motivating a good theory, it's thus a clear constraint that the resulting theory be consistent. However, it's one thing to *block* an inconsistency, and another to *diagnose* it. Sam Roberts (MSb) has recently identified the following challenge:

> Some conditions, like the condition of being non-self-membered, fail to determine sets. Nevertheless, set theory tells us that many conditions do determine sets. The axiom of pairing, for example, says that the condition of being *a* or *b* determines a set whenever *a* and *b* are sets. We are thus faced with a challenge: to provide an account of the dividing line between the conditions that determine sets and those that don't which explains why there are many of the sets there are – enough for the purposes of set theory – but not problematic sets like the Russell set. (p. 2)[41]

Roberts refers to this problem of identifying which conditions do/do not determine sets and explaining why as *the explanatory challenge*. On this basis we can identify the following desideratum on a conception of set:

Paradox Diagnosis Respond to the explanatory challenge: Explain why the paradoxical collections aren't sets and which conditions do (and do not) determine sets.[42]

To sum up: We want to find a conception of set of that provides a picture of the sets exhibiting **Naturalness**, is rich enough to provide an **Interpretation** for a good theory of sets (allowing us also to fulfil the goals of Section 2), and provides us with a **Paradox Diagnosis** by responding to the explanatory challenge and telling us *which* conditions are problematic, and *why* they don't determine sets. In a moment (Section 5.3) we'll see a further desideratum – what I'll call **Capture** – that applies specifically to *iterative* conceptions of set. Before we get there though, I want to consider a couple of more coarse-grained approaches. Examining them will help us see better the ways in which iterative conceptions can make progress.

---

[41] See also Roberts (2016), pp. 9–11.

[42] Closely related is the challenge of making a *metaphysical* distinction between sets and proper classes (e.g. by identifying different ontological kinds). See Maddy (1983) and Barton (2017), ch. IV.

4.2 The Logical and Combinatorial Conceptions of Set

We can begin by considering the the distinction between:

Definition 14 (Informal) The *logical conception* of set holds that sets correspond to *well-defined predicates*.

and:

Definition 15 (Informal) The *combinatorial conception* of set holds that sets correspond to *acceptable pluralities* (possibly without there being any non-trivial defining predicate).[43]

Clearly, these conceptions are pretty rough-and-ready, certainly they are not fully precise. As we'll see shortly, each admits of multiple different sharpenings. Moreover, we might not think that the distinction between the two is sharp – perhaps there are some conceptions of set that borrow a little from each.[44] We'll see one such conception – the *constructibilist conception* – in just a moment, and there may well be others.[45] Still, I think they're useful to think about as they highlight the following:

(1) When faced with mutually inconsistent principles about the sets, we can very naturally move forward by developing a conception that rejects (at least) one of them.

(2) Conceptions are often *imprecise* and/or *underspecified*, and further development of the conceptions may be needed for progress.

Let's examine these two points in more detail.

4.3 Responding to Paradox and Sharpening Conceptions

The consideration of the distinction between the logical and combinatorial conceptions of set indicates the following *germ* of a response to the paradoxes. Many ways of making the logical conception precise will hold that the predicate $x = x$ is 'well-defined'. Thus, under the logical conception, **Universality** is likely to be validated and **Indefinite Extensibility** violated. Conversely,

---

[43] Incurvati (2020), p. 31, talks about the combinatorial conception as holding that sets are characterised via 'reference to their members'. I wish to avoid awkward metasemantic issues surrounding *reference*, and so I've used pluralities instead.

[44] See Incurvati (2020) (especially section 1.8) for further discussion and references.

[45] For example, there are versions of *predicativism* that seem to combine a notion of 'good' definitions with successive set formation from available pluralities. See Linnebo and Shapiro (2023) for such a view.

versions of the combinatorial conception will make the notion of 'acceptable plurality' precise in a variety of ways, and in doing so can make it the case that the plurality of all sets is not an 'acceptable plurality'. So it is **Universality**, and not **Indefinite Extensibility**, that is often identified as the culprit. We thus seem to have the *beginnings* of a **Paradox Diagnosis**; explanations of what the sets *are like* might be used to explain why it is that one of the two principles fail. So, when faced with paradox, an attractive move is to *modify* our conception of set in response, attacking one of the two conflicting principles.[46]

Moreover, these two conceptions correspond to reasonably **Natural** conceptions. Returning to the example of my collection of beer coasters: let's suppose I want to think about the set of all objects in this collection. I may talk about the relevant set of beer coasters as the set of everything that is both a beer coaster and currently in a certain shoebox in my bedroom (thereby using the logical conception). But there is also a certain plurality of objects – the individuals $b_1, ..., b_n$ considered in the plural – each of which just happens to be a beer coaster in that particular shoebox. And it seems that there's no obstacle to me considering the set of *them* (thereby thinking of the relevant set combinatorially).

Though useful both for beginning to sharpen our conception of set and providing a preliminary classification, the logical and combinatorial conceptions are still rather imprecise in a number of ways, and this leads to them being *defective* (without further sharpening). For example, let's consider **Interpretation**. What formal theory is motivated by either the logical or combinatorial conception alone? There seems to be little that one can say when thinking about either as stated earlier. We first need explanations of what *well-defined predicates* are, or what it is to be an *acceptable plurality*. And without a formal theory we can't achieve lots of the nice goals from Section 2.

This brings us on to our second point: When faced with some defectiveness in our conception of set, it's attractive to develop the conception in order to make progress. This could be in the face of paradox, but we also might be galvanised to do so by given other deficiencies (e.g. a failure to address **Interpretation**). For example, in order to improve the logical conception, we need to say what 'well-defined' means. There are a number of ways of doing this.

---

[46] It should be noted that this diagnosis isn't completely neat. One might make the case that there are logical conceptions of set that violate **Universality** and combinatorial conceptions that violate **Indefinite Extensibility**. Incurvati (2020), for example, characterises the limitation of size conception as logical, but that doesn't allow for all the self-identical sets forming a set. It's not clear to me that the limitation of size conception is in fact logical, but in any case we can view those (more precise) conceptions that validate **Universality** as the relevant contrast cases for what we're doing here. We'll see throughout this Element that the classifications amongst the conceptions might not be sharp.

One (the *stratified conception*) holds that there are certain formulas that are appropriately stratified, and that comprehension should be restricted to these formulas.[47] Another (the *iterative property conception*) holds that there is a way of iteratively individuating those formulas that can be used in comprehension (this is the approach of the property theories of Fine (2005), Linnebo (2006), and Roberts (MSa)). On each of these, as it happens, the predicate $x = x$ is well-defined and individuates an extension, validating acceptance of **Universality** over **Indefinite Extensibility**.

The combinatorial conception, by contrast, needs to make precise what it is for a plurality to be *acceptable*. One way is to say that some sets are acceptable if and only if they can be depicted as part of a particular kind of graph (the *graph conception*). This conception also conforms to our earlier diagnosis, validating **Indefinite Extensibility** but rejecting **Universality**.[48] *Iterative conceptions* (the foci of this Element) also refute **Universality** whilst accepting **Indefinite Extensibility**. They hold that a plurality is acceptable if it can be formed from other sets using set-construction methods. Let's now turn to these conceptions.

5 Iterative Conceptions: First Examples

In this section, I want to present the emergence of several conceptions of set and the eventual rise of what I'll call the 'strong iterative conception'. We'll see that this idea can be formalised *modally* and there's a *close affinity* with ZFC. This conception also performs wonderfully with respect to the desiderata we've considered. But I also want to indicate that the strong iterative conception, though it may be the default, isn't the only conception on the market.

---

[47] The stratified conception is proposed by Quine (1937) and its history is nicely outlined in Incurvati (2020). One starts with the following definition:

Definition 16 A formula ϕ in the language of set theory is *stratified* if and only if there is an assignment of natural numbers to variables such that:

(i) For any subformula of ϕ the form $x = y$, the natural number assigned to x is the same as the number assigned to y.
(ii) For any subformula of ϕ the form $x \in y$, the natural number assigned to y is one greater than the number assigned to x.

By restricting comprehension to stratified formulas we obtain a system known as NF.

[48] Since we won't discuss this much, we'll set it aside, but see Incurvati (2020), ch. 7 for details. The relevant notion is an *accessible pointed graph*, a kind of directed graph where there's a distinguished top node (this is the 'pointed' part of the definition, and you can think of this 'point' as the set we want to code), the edges code the membership relations, with accessibility meaning that it's possible to reach each node of the graph by some finite chain of edges starting from the point.

5.1 Some Iterative Conceptions of Set

We'll consider a kind of combinatorial conception known as the *iterative* conception. We'll keep things rough and imprecise to begin with (this imprecision will be helpful later when we separate out different versions of it):

Definition 17 (Informal) The *iterative conception* of set holds that sets are formed in stages, and new sets are formed from old by collecting together sets formed at previous stages. There are no other sets than those found at the stages.

The rough idea can be filled out as follows. We (or better yet a suitably idealised being) start at an initial stage with some initially given collection of objects. These could be a bunch of non-sets (often called *Urelemente*), or some antecedently given sets that we take to be acceptable (e.g. the empty set).[49] We then begin forming new sets out of what we have using some given operations, and in this way obtain the sets. So long as our operations guarantee that new sets can always be formed, we have an explanation of why **Indefinite Extensibility** holds and **Universality** fails – there will never be a stage at which we can use an operation to collect all the sets into a set.

The iterative conception of set as I've given it can in fact be split into two conceptions, a strong one and a weak one:[50]

Definition 18 (Informal) The *strong iterative conception* of set holds that sets are obtained in stages. At each additional stage we form *every possible subplurality* of the current stage as a set. There are no other sets beyond those obtained this way.

Definition 19 (Informal) The *weak iterative conception* of set holds that sets are formed in stages. Sets are formed by collecting together sets existing at previous stages using some set-construction methods. We leave it open whether or not we get every possible subplurality of what we have at a stage as a set immediately after the current one. There are no other sets beyond those obtained this way.

I want to suggest that the weak iterative conception is really *prior* to the strong iterative conception (conceptually, if not chronologically). Key to the weak iterative conception are:

---

[49]　Depending on what set-construction methods we allow, we have to be careful that we don't start with a proper class. If we do, some modification is needed; see, for example, Menzel (1986) and Menzel (2014).

[50]　This distinction emerged in discussion with Chris Scambler, and I'm grateful to him for the suggestion of separating out the two.

(i) A description of what counts as a starting domain.
(ii) A description of some construction methods for forming new sets from old.

The strong iterative conception says (i) can be any set of objects, but the empty set will do, and (ii) that the operations that form new sets consist solely of powerset (i.e. taking all possible subsets). (**Note:** As we'll see later, we also take unions at limits. No new sets are formed in the limit, however, it just consists in 'bundling together' everything we constructed previously.) It thus *sharpens* the weak iterative conception; there are other methods of set-construction that we might have chosen. Let's see an example of the difference by going into more detail on each.

The strong iterative conception is perhaps the simplest version of the weak iterative conception, so we'll explore it first. It is also perhaps the 'default' version – as of this writing, if you put the terms 'iterative conception of set' into a search engine, you'll get back results about the strong iterative conception. Whilst I won't enter into historical details too much here, an excellent description of its emergence is available in Kanamori (2007), and Button (2021a) impressively charts its formal (stage-theoretic) development.

Often the idea of the strong iterative conception is formalised within ZFC with the following definition using ordinal numbers:

Definition 20 *The Cumulative Hierarchy of Sets* or *V* is defined as follows:[51]

(i) $V_0 = \emptyset$
(ii) $V_{\alpha+1} = \mathcal{P}(V_\alpha)$, where $\alpha + 1$ is a successor ordinal.
(iii) $V_\lambda = \bigcup_{\alpha<\lambda} V_\lambda$ (if λ is a limit ordinal)

The structure of the V_α thus captures the idea that we take all possible subsets at each additional stage (i.e. iterate powerset) and collect them together at limits (i.e. take a union). The often given visual representation is provided in Figure 1.

The weak iterative conception is in some ways less well studied than the strong iterative conception, possibly partly because the latter is seen as the default. However, since the weak iterative conception is more general and will be important later, it will be worth getting it on the table.

---

[51] For simplicity, I am giving the version for pure sets; if you want to include Urelemente, then clause (i) should be replaced with $V_0 = \{x|\ ‘x$ is an Urelement'$\}$, and clause (ii) by $V_{\alpha+1} = \mathcal{P}(V_\alpha) \cup V_\alpha$. The situation can get tricky depending on what Urelmente one allows, see Menzel (1986), Menzel (2014), and Button (2021a) for discussion.

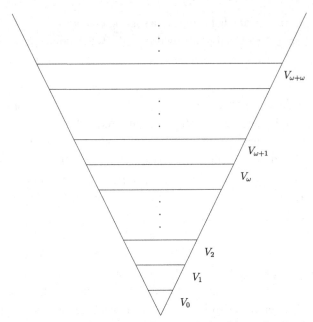

Figure 1 A visual representation of the cumulative hierarchy. Each additional stage is obtained by applying the powerset operation, and at limit stages we union together the previous stages. The figure contains only a tiny fraction of the beginnings of the hierarchy; as we go further and further, each ordinal α indexes some V_α, and $\omega + \omega$ is a comparatively small countable ordinal.

We'll see a few examples of the weak iterative conception in this Element, but some will have to wait until we have a couple of set-theoretic constructions under our belt. For now, here's an easier example to get a feel for it. Suppose we want to build the hereditarily finite sets (i.e. finite sets that are built up out of only finite sets all the way down – formally we say that the empty set is hereditarily finite, and any other set is hereditarily finite just in case it is finite and all its members are hereditarily finite). In standard set theory, we can get these sets just by taking powersets from the empty set (i.e. moving up through each V_n for every natural number n). But there are other ways we might build these sets. Suppose we individuate sets in stages by starting with the empty set at stage 0 and forming at stage $n + 1$ all sets of size at most n. As we continue through all the stages up to ω (the first infinite stage), we'll eventually get every hereditarily finite set. But we won't get every possible subset at a successor stage. For instance, you can check that stage 4 has eight members, so you'll miss out some subsets of stage 4 when moving to stage 5 (you'll have to wait until stage 8 before you can form all subsets of stage 4). So, this procedure is weakly but *not* strongly iterative – there are possible sets that don't get formed at the next stage.

We can also have processes that are not even *linearly ordered*, for instance by having two or more set forming operations. For example, let the operation **Even!** form the subsets of a stage with an even number of elements. The other **Odd!** forms the odd numbered subsets of a given stage. By interleaving **Even!** and **Odd!** finitely many times we can get any hereditarily finite set. But the process is not linearly ordered; for instance, we could choose to do **Even!** a bunch of times in a row. One doesn't even have a guarantee that you get every hereditarily finite set using these processes (say if you just head off only iterating **Even!** over and over again).

There are more mathematically interesting kinds of weak iterative conception. Here's a more difficult (but important) example:

Definition 21 (Informal) The *constructibilist conception* holds that sets are formed in stages. At subsequent stages we form into sets those pluralities of previous stages that are *definable* (i.e. can be picked out by a formula) over that stage. There are no other sets beyond those obtained this way.

Is conception weakly or strongly iterative? We can show that there are versions of it that are only *weakly* iterative.

✻ Often set theorists will talk about the *constructible universe* (or L) and *constructible hierarchy*. L is formed by taking *definable* powersets. A subset x of the domain of a structure $\mathfrak{M}$ is *definable over* $\mathfrak{M}$ if and only if x is the unique set containing all and only the y in the domain of $\mathfrak{M}$ satisfying $\phi(y)$ (in $\mathfrak{M}$) for some condition $\phi(y)$ in the language of $\mathfrak{M}$.[a] For a structure $\mathfrak{M}$, let's call the collection of all such $\mathfrak{M}$-definable subsets $Def(\mathfrak{M})$. Then L can be defined as:

Definition 22 The *constructible hierarchy* (or just L) is defined as follows:

    (i) $L_0 = \emptyset$
    (ii) $L_{\alpha+1} = Def(L_\alpha)$ for successor ordinal $\alpha + 1$.
    (iii) $L_\lambda = \bigcup_{\alpha < \lambda} L_\alpha$ for limit ordinal λ.

The axiom that every set is constructible (i.e. 'For every x there is an α such that $x \in L_\alpha$') is called the *Axiom of Constructibility* or $V = L$.

Now the constructible hierarchy clearly satisfies the weak iterative conception and the constructibilist conception. But it *doesn't* satisfy the strong iterative conception. This is because often new subsets of previous levels get formed as we climb. For example, new subsets of ω coding new real numbers get formed as we move up through the first few stages above L_ω. To see this, note that a *satisfaction predicate* for L_α is definable over $L_{\alpha+1}$, and above V_ω these will code new subsets of natural numbers. This phenomenon (the slow growth of L) is quite general. Since there are only as many formulas as there are parameters available (the usual formula-building operations are trivial at infinite cardinals) we have that the cardinality of L_α is the same as the cardinality of $L_{\alpha+1}$ for every α (in stark contrast to the V_α-hierarchy where $V_{\alpha+1}$ is *always* bigger than V_α). So, the L_α hierarchy does not satisfy the strong iterative conception; there are possible subsets that don't get picked up when we move to a subsequent stage. I represent this visually in Figure 2.

Moreover, we could make the iteration more fine-grained and non-linearly ordered. I could take each *formula* to provide its *own* set-forming operation, and think of successively forming subsets *for specific formulas*, instead of taking the whole definable powerset. This would still qualify as weakly iterative.

Note: Sometimes you can *recover* a version of the strong iterative conception from the weak one. In the case of our *n*-sized-set-forming operation, we could eventually recover the V_n-hierarchy if we wait long enough. This holds for the L_α-hierarchy too; for example, if L satisfies ZFC, it can *recover* its own version of the V_α-hierarchy.[a]

However, one can still see the difference between the two hierarchies, even when we assume that V is equal to L. For, even if ZFC holds, it is not the case that $V_\alpha = L_\alpha$ for every α. Rather the L_α-hierarchy grows slower than the V_α-hierarchy, it is just that the L_α-hierarchy can 'catch up' at limit stages.

---

[a] This is fiddly to formulate. See chapter 3, section 5 of Drake (1974).

Remark 23 An important but somewhat orthogonal side remark: I mentioned earlier that the combinatorial and logical conceptions of set were pretty rough-and-ready. I think that the constructibilist conception provides a good example to showcase how the two might be neither neatly separable nor incompatible. On the one hand, the constructibilist conception is clearly combinatorial, we have an explanation of when a plurality is available; namely when it is defin-able after iterating the formation of definable powersets. But notice also that under the constructibilist conception the existence of sets is *intimately* tied to defining conditions – given the formation of some set x, it must comprise

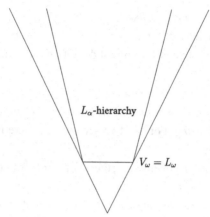

L_α-hierarchy

$V_\omega = L_\omega$

Figure 2 The constructible universe sitting inside the cumulative hierarchy. In the case where every set is constructible, we still do not have $V_\alpha = L_\alpha$ for every α; rather, the L_α-hierarchy can catch up at limit stages before continuing to grow slower than the V_α-hierarchy.

exactly the satisfiers of some condition from a previous stage. So it's very unclear whether it's correct to characterise the constructibilist conception as either combinatorial or logical; it seems to borrow ideas from each.

To sum up: There are multiple sharpenings of the weak iterative conception. One is the strong iterative conception. But others (e.g. the constructibilist conception) are mathematically interesting and not strongly iterative. Clearly, some of these conceptions can be used to motivate certain axioms (for example, the constructibilist conception motivates the axiom that every set is constructible). But can we lend formal precision to this idea of motivating theories? Let's see how this can be done with the *strong* iterative conception.

5.2 ⚄ Modal Set Theory and the Strong Iterative Conception

We want our conceptions of set to motivate virtuous theories. Later (Section 8) we'll see how versions of the weak iterative conception other than the constructibilist conception can be used to do just this. For now, we'll focus on the 'default' strong iterative conception and ZFC. In particular, I'll:

(1) Explain ZFC set theory.
(2) Show how ZFC can be motivated on the basis of a modal axiomatisation of the strong iterative conception.

So, let's start by setting up ZFC:

Definition 24 *Zermelo–Fraenkel Set Theory with the Axiom of Choice* (ZFC) is formulated in the language of set theory $\mathscr{L}_\in$. It comprises the following axioms (we just give informal statements; formal definitions are available in many set theory textbooks):

(i) *Axiom of Extensionality.* Sets with the same members are identical.

(ii) *Axiom of Pairing.* For any two sets x and y there is a set containing just x and y.

(iii) *Axiom of Union.* For any set x, there is a set of all members of members of x.

(iv) *Powerset Axiom.* For any set x, there is a set of all subsets of x.

(v) *Axiom of Foundation.* Every set contains an element that is disjoint from it. The axiom both rules out self-membered sets and also the existence of infinite descending membership chains.

(vi) *Axiom of Infinity.* There's a non-empty set x such that for any member y of x there is another member z of x such that y is a member of z. (This guarantees that there's an infinite set.)

(vii) *Axiom of Choice.* (AC) For any non-empty set of pairwise-disjoint non-empty sets, there is a set that picks one member from each. (**Note:** ZFC without AC is just denoted by "ZF". In the presence of ZF this is equivalent to the **Well-Ordering Principle** that every set can be well-ordered.)

(viii) *Axiom Scheme of Replacement.* If a formula $\phi(x,y)$ is function-like (i.e. for any x, there is exactly one y such that $\phi(x,y)$), then the image of any particular set under $\phi(x,y)$ is also a set.

The following are provable ZFC, normally using Replacement. They will be relevant later when we consider dropping the Powerset Axiom (in that context, they can't be proved from Replacement) and so we'll include them as part of ZFC:

(ix) *Axiom Scheme of Separation.* If $\phi(x)$ is a formula in one free variable x, then if y is a set, then there's a set of all the x in y such that $\phi(x)$ (i.e. $\{z \mid z \in y \wedge \phi(z)\}$ exists).

(x) *Axiom Scheme of Collection.* For any formula $\phi(x,y)$ in two free variables, if $\phi(x,y)$ defines a relation, and for some set a and for every $x \in a$ there is always a y ϕ-related to x, then there is a set z 'collecting' together at least one 'ϕ-witness' for every $x \in a$. Since this axiom scheme may be a little less familiar, we'll include its formal statement:

$$(\forall a)\big((\forall x \in a)(\exists y)\phi(x,y) \rightarrow (\exists b)(\forall x \in a)(\exists y \in b)\phi(x,y)\big)$$

As noted earlier (Section 2) ZFC is a very nice theory of sets with many theoretical virtues. But can it be motivated using the iterative conception?

There are different ways to do this. One way is to axiomatise the notion of a stage *directly*.[52] Whilst this meshes very well with the 'stage-theoretic' terminology employed earlier, I want to take a slightly different approach here. Instead, we'll think of the iterative conception as describing how new sets can be formed from old using set-construction methods, and in this way giving us a kind of *modal* framework. There are a few reasons for this choice that I'll just *briefly* mention. First, the modal approach makes some questions regarding **Interpretation** a little more tractable using existing technology (we'll see how shortly). Second, thinking of things modally provides an easy integration with other areas of philosophy. For example, if we think that sets are specified as part of a modal framework, then the nature of this framework and the modalities employed may well be of interest to the modal metaphysician.[53] Third, there is an easy way to view these modal theories in stage-theoretic terms – we can simply think of the corresponding worlds as the stages and our chosen set-constuction methods as providing the accessibility relation. Fourth, it's the modal approach to the weak iterative conception that has been better developed in the literature thus far (indeed, developing properly stage-theoretic accounts of the weak iterative conception will be left as an open question in Section 10).

This said, this choice is *controversial*.[54] We might think that the modal approach deviates somewhat from the stage-theoretic account of the iterative conception, suggesting different kinds of philosophical question. Moreover, as we'll explore later (Section 10), there's some substantial open questions about how well the modal approach formalises either the weak or strong iterative conceptions.[55] For now I'll put these questions to one side, but I don't want to overstate my position. Iterative conceptions are informal accounts of the nature of the sets. There are *choices* to be made in how to formalise these ideas. Some may be better than others, and there is significant philosophical work to be done in contrasting the different approaches.

The idea to view the iterative conception modally is relatively old, going back to Parsons (1983), but has been fruitfully applied recently. In particular, Linnebo (2013) shows how one can give modal axioms motivating ZFC. Giving

---

[52] See Button (2021a) for a recent article on the state of the art.

[53] A friendly introduction to these issues is available in Menzel (2021).

[54] I am grateful to Davide Sutto and Chris Scambler for some discussion of this point.

[55] For example, as we'll see, some modal approaches yield non-well-founded accessibility relations. But let's defer a more thorough examination of this issue until later.

the full details would take up too much space, but a flavour of the approach will be useful.[56]

As is clear from the way I've presented the iterative conception informally, we'll want to talk about reifying pluralities into sets, and for this Linnebo uses a plural logic. Really though, any extensional second-order variables would do. Since much of the literature (e.g. Scambler (2021)) follows this convention of using plurals, we'll stick with it. Again we'll leave the plural logic relatively informal; the reader wishing to see a concise presentation of the details is directed to Linnebo (2014) or Oliver and Smiley (2013) for textbook treatments. Plural logic has new variables xx that range over 'some things' (e.g. the books on my table), a binary relation symbol $\prec$ (where $x \prec xx$ is to be read as "x is one of the xx"), with the expected definition of well-formed formula. We'll denote the language obtained by adding these resources to $\mathscr{L}_\in$ by "$\mathscr{L}_{\in,\prec}$". We'll routinely abuse singularisation and speak of "a plurality" (a standard move in this field).

For our plural axioms (here we're mostly following the presentation in Scambler (2021)) we'll take the following:

Definition 25 *Plural logic* (over set theory) has as axioms (we'll give these axioms informally, see Linnebo (2018), ch. 12 for the formal details):

(i) A principle of extensionality for plurals (that if two pluralities xx and yy comprise the same things, then anything that holds of the xx also holds of the yy and vice versa).[57]

(ii) Additionally, *impredicative* plural logic has the following **Impredicative Comprehension Scheme**:

$$\exists xx \forall y (y \prec xx \leftrightarrow \phi(y))$$

for any ϕ in $\mathscr{L}_{\in,\prec}$ not containing xx free.

(iii) *Predicative* plural logic does not contain the **Impredicative Comprehension Scheme** but rather has the following **Predicative Comprehension Scheme**:

$$\exists xx \forall y (y \prec xx \leftrightarrow \phi(y))$$

for any ϕ in $\mathscr{L}_{\in,\prec}$ not containing xx free and not containing any plural quantifiers.

---

[56] Details can be found in Linnebo (2013) and Scambler (2021), and different modal approaches are given by Studd (2013) and Button (2021b).

[57] I'm suppressing some subtleties here about how one formulates the extensionality axiom; see Roberts (2022) for details.

We then need a background modal logic to talk about what's possible after constructing new sets. For this we'll add a modal operator $\Diamond$ to $\mathscr{L}_{\in, <}$ to get a language $\mathscr{L}^{\Diamond}_{\in, <}$, with well-formed formulas as normal. We'll also use the modal operator $\Box$, and in this context $\Box\phi$ can be treated as shorthand for $\neg\Diamond\neg\phi$. For modal axioms we'll use:

Definition 26 Classical S4 is the modal logic with the operator $\Diamond$ and the axioms:

(i) The necessity of identity and distinctness (these are sometimes optional, but we'll include them):
- $x = y \rightarrow \Box(x = y)$
- $x \neq y \rightarrow \Box(x \neq y)$

(ii) K: $\Box(\phi \rightarrow \psi) \rightarrow (\Box\phi \rightarrow \Box\psi)$ (this holds for any normal modal logic).

(iii) T: $\phi \rightarrow \Diamond\phi$ (this holds if the accessibility relation is reflexive).

(iv) 4: $\Diamond\Diamond\phi \rightarrow \Diamond\phi$ (holds if the accessibility relation is transitive).

To obtain S4.2 we add:

(v) G (sometimes called .2): $\Diamond\Box\phi \rightarrow \Box\Diamond\phi$ (holds if the accessibility relation is directed).

The logic S4.3 is obtained by adding:

(vi) .3: $(\Diamond\phi \wedge \Diamond\psi) \rightarrow \Diamond((\Diamond\phi \wedge \psi) \vee (\phi \wedge \Diamond\psi))$ (holds if the accessibility relation is linear).

Throughout, we will also assume:

(vii) The Converse Barcan Formula (CBF): $\exists x \Diamond\phi \rightarrow \Diamond\exists x\phi$ (this can be thought of as capturing the idea that domains only grow).

Because we have S4.2 you can think of the space of worlds as a kind of branching time structure, but where you can always bring together any two possibilities (this is the content of the G/.2 axiom). Thus $\Box\phi$ can be thought of as saying "in all future worlds ϕ" and $\Diamond\phi$ as "there is a future world such that ϕ". And S4.3 makes it so that there's a kind of inevitability to how the possibilities unfold.[58]

Before we give our modal axioms, we should clarify how we'll interpret *non*-modal set theory. Mostly mathematicians will just want to work with a non-modal axiomatisation of sets, without paying attention to finicky modal details about how the sets are formed. So we can ask: Is there a way of interpreting non-modal set theories in $\mathscr{L}_\in$ into our modal language $\mathscr{L}^{\Diamond}_{\in, <}$? Given the iterative

---

[58] It should be noted that the converses of (v) and (vii) do not hold (i.e. there are frames that are not directed that satisfy G/.2, and non-linear frames satisfying .3).

conception, how should we interpret the 'usual' quantifiers ∀ and ∃? Well, one natural thought is that ∀xφ should hold if, no matter how you form sets, φ will *always* hold, and ∃xφ tells you that you *can* go on to form sets such that φ. We can then provide:

Definition 27 Given a sentence φ in $\mathcal{L}_\in$, the *potentialist translation of* φ (denoted "$φ^\lozenge$") is obtained by replacing every universal quantifier "∀" by "□∀", and every existential quantifier "∃" by "◇∃".

We can then define a version of the modal axioms that is extracted from Linnebo (2013):[59]

Definition 28 Linnebo (2013), Linnebo (2018) (here we follow Scambler's (2021) presentation) Lin is the following theory in $\mathcal{L}^\lozenge_{\in,<}$:

(i) Classical first-order predicate logic.

(ii) Impredicative plural logic.

(iii) Classical S4.2 with the Converse Barcan Formula added.[60]

(iv) The Axiom of Foundation (rendered as normal using solely resources from $\mathcal{L}_\in$).[61]

(v) Extensionality (again using solely resources from $\mathcal{L}_\in$).

(vi) **Modal Collapse.** The principle that any things (at a stage) could form a set:

$$□∀xx◇∃y□∀x(z \in y \leftrightarrow z < xx)$$

(vii) Stability axioms for < and ∈ (these mirror the necessity of identity/distinctness):[62]

- $x \in y \rightarrow □(x \in y)$

---

[59] I'm basically following the presentation in Scambler (2021), with a few extra tweaks that will be useful later. Scambler uses "L" to denote Lin, so I've opted for syntax that avoids possible confusion of Lin with the constructible hierarchy *L*. Strictly speaking, Linnebo (2013) doesn't include the plural version of the Axiom of Choice (he is looking for interpretation with ZF) but Scambler (2021) does (but he throws it in as part of the plural logic; I include it as a hybrid plural-cum-set-theoretic axiom). With these systems you get as much Choice out as you're willing to throw in, and since we're primarily interested in ZFC in this Element, I'm happy to throw it in.

[60] Normally the Converse Barcan Formula comes for free (one must take steps to block it), see Linnebo (2018), p. 207. I've added it for the sake of explicitness and making the 'growing domains' conception of potentialism clear. I'll make no further mention of this complication.

[61] Another nice option here is to use ∈-induction. Thanks to Øystein Linnebo for some discussion of this point.

[62] It should be noted that a choice point here concerns whether to use the quantified or free-variable forms of these axioms, since the free-variable versions seem stronger. Thanks to Chris Scambler for some discussion of this point.

- $x \notin y \rightarrow \Box(x \notin y)$
- $x < yy \rightarrow \Box(x < yy)$
- $x \nprec yy \rightarrow \Box(x \nprec yy)$

(viii) Two principles of plural definiteness:

- **Plural Membership Definiteness** is given by the following scheme:

$$(\forall x < yy)\Box\phi(x) \rightarrow \Box(\forall x < yy)\phi(x)$$

- **Subplurality Definiteness**: Say that $xx \leq yy$ holds just in case the xx are a subplurality of the yy, that is, for every x such that $x < xx$ we have $x < yy$. Then the **Subplurality Definiteness** scheme states that:

$$(\forall xx \leq yy)\Box\phi(xx) \rightarrow \Box(\forall xx \leq yy)\phi(xx).$$

(ix) **Modal Infinity.** The axiom that there could be some things comprising all and only the possible natural numbers.

(x) **Modal Powerclass.** The axiom that there could be some things that are all and only the possible subsets of a given set.

(xi) **Modal Replacement.** Every potentialist translation of the Replacement Scheme of ZFC.

(xii) **Plural Choice.** A plural version of the Axiom of Choice 'For any pairwise-disjoint non-empty sets xx, there are some things yy that comprise exactly one element from each member of the xx'.[63]

Together, these get us some way to providing a modal axiomatisation of the strong iterative conception. Let's discuss the **Naturalness** of these axioms. Of course the extent to which a modal set theory is natural and/or not ad hoc will likely be somewhat imprecise and a matter of degree. Given any set x, there could be (by **Modal Powerclass**) a plurality of all possible subsets of x. Using **Modal Collapse**, this plurality can then be reified into a set. Thus there's a clear picture of how the sets are formed – our set-construction method turns pluralities of the domain into sets. I'll refer to such methods as '**Reify!** commands', and talk about using **Reify!** to turn pluralities into sets.

From this picture, we also get a **Paradox Diagnosis**. It explains why **Indefinite Extensibility** holds and **Universality** fails – the universal set never gets formed because at no stage is there a plurality of all possible sets; we can

---

[63] Strictly speaking, Linnebo does not include AC, but I'm happy to throw it in. Some other authors (e.g. Studd (2013)) do so. Nothing hangs on it for the results we have here, other than the fact that if Lin is run without a form of AC, the that gets interpreted will also not include AC (it will be ZF rather than ZFC).

always form something new. In particular, the Russell plurality of all non-self-membered sets at a world will be formed (via **Reify!**) as a set at a later world.

Unfortunately, we don't *quite* yet get the full strong iterative conception. Although the modal set theory Lin axiomatises an *uncountabilist* conception of set (in that it implies that there could be a set that is necessarily uncountable), the axiomatisation does not *exactly* correspond to the formation of the universe via powersets and union. The problem lies in the fact that though **Modal Powerclass** and **Modal Collapse** entail that the full powerset of a set could exist, there is no guarantee that it is formed immediately. It might take some time and there might be some intermediate worlds before the relevant powerset appears.[64]

Though we won't go into too much detail on this, here's how you can enforce the strong iterative conception. Whilst I am not aware of any axiom in $\mathscr{L}_{\in,<}^{\Diamond}$ that guarantees that the powerset gets formed immediately, one can use *bimodal* operators to enforce the *immediate* collapse of *every* possible plurality of a world into a set. James Studd provides one such axiomatisation (in Studd, 2013), with subsequent examination and a further approach by Tim Button (in Button (2021b); I'll largely follow Button). Here we have two modal operators ◆ and ◇ that capture the 'timelike' feature of forming sets; ◆ϕ is intended to mean that it was the case that ϕ (or "previously ϕ" if you like), and ◇ϕ is intended to mean that it will be the case that ϕ (or "eventually ϕ"), with the usual dual necessity operators. Tweaks to the modal logic are needed to incorporate these resources (in particular Button and Studd both work in a free logic) but we won't dwell on that here. The important point is that one can use these modal operators to ensure that every plurality is formed into a set at subsequent worlds via an axiom asserting that if every possible ϕ existed earlier, then there is a set comprising exactly the ϕs. In the context of plural logic (or a suitable second-order logic) we immediately get the result that every plurality xx forms a set at all worlds after each of its members exists.[65]

For the sake of simplicity (and in particular avoiding the complications of free logic) I'll stick with Lin, but we could run the same points using Button or Studd's systems too. Moreover, the V_α can be used to obtain a Kripke frame

---

64 ⚡ In fact one can (with a little work) obtain a Kripke model for Lin from the L_α of a model of ZFC, and, as noted before, the L_α don't get you the strong iterative conception. See Barton (MSb) for discussion and a sketch.

65 ⚡ Formally: If $E(x)$ is the relevant existence predicate in free logic, one can formalise the claim as follows (we use the formulation in second-order logic rather than plural logic, as in Button (2021b)):

$$(\forall F)(\forall x\colon F)\blacklozenge E(x) \to (\exists a)(\forall x)(F(x) \leftrightarrow x \in a)$$

for Lin (as we'll discuss shortly), so Lin is satisfied under the strong iterative conception (even if there are other conceptions that satisfy Lin).

5.3 Mirroring and Capture

Let's now look at **Interpretation**. The core concept will be the idea of *Mirroring Theorems*. These tell you how you can go between the modal theories and the non-modal theories favoured by mathematicians. In particular we can show:

Theorem 29 *Linnebo (2010), Linnebo (2013)* ZFC *proves* ϕ *if and only if* Lin *proves* $\phi^\diamond$.

This theorem shows that the modal idea of reifying all pluralities into sets at a stage (and continuing this into the transfinite) motivates ZFC concerning the sets. And as we noted in Section 2, ZFC is a very nice set theory! Moreover, it shows how Lin is strongly faithful to 'normal' set theory under the potentialist translation.[66]

Interestingly, the relationship goes back the other way too. Earlier, we mentioned that the strong iterative conception suggests that the universe is formed via the V_α-hierarchy. But one can also show:

Theorem 30 *Linnebo (2013) Over a model of* ZFC, *the* V_α *under* $\subseteq$ *provide a model for* Lin.[67]

This shows that not only does Lin motivate ZFC, but if you accept ZFC then you can also get a model for the modal set-construction methods axiomatised by Lin. This shows that although Lin doesn't perfectly capture the notion of the strong iterative conception, it certainly fits very well with it.

One final piece of the puzzle ties everything together:

Theorem 31 *(ZF) For every set x there is an ordinal* α *such that* $x \in V_\alpha$.

---

[66] Indeed, this result can be strengthened to apply to very weak theories, Tim Button (in Button (2021a) and Button (2021b)) has shown that one can go back and forth between *tremendously* weak (i) theories of sets, (ii) theories of stages, and (iii) modal stage theories (the theories in question do not even imply there *are* any sets!).

[67] Specifically a Kripke frame validating S4.3. In order to interpret the plural logic, strictly speaking we should think of worlds as pairs of the form $(V_\alpha, \mathcal{P}(V_\alpha))$, with $\prec$ just interpreted by $\in$.

This theorem shows you that not only does ZFC allow you to *define* the V_α, but you can prove that *every* set is contained therein. I think that this highlights the following desideratum on modal axiomatisations of conceptions of set:

Capture Let $T^\Diamond$ be a modal theory of sets interpreting a non-modal theory T via the potentialist translation. Then we say that $T^\Diamond$ satisfies **Capture** if and only if, given a model M of T, we have a general way of extracting a Kripke frame $K_{T^\Diamond}^M \models T^\Diamond$ from M such that for every $x \in M$ there is a world $W \in K_{T^\Diamond}^M$ such that $x \in W$.[68]

The statement of **Capture** is a little complicated. But the core point is the following: Not only does our modal theory (in this case Lin) motivate a nice non-modal theory of sets (namely ZFC), but our non-modal theory (ZFC) also 'thinks' that there is a model of the modal theory (Lin) such that every set lives in said model. Perhaps it would be too strong to say that they are sides of the same coin, but they certainly pair very well.[69]

5.4 Preliminary Conclusions

We're now in a position where (i) the strong iterative conception is **Natural** (giving us a clear picture of what the sets are like), (ii) it gives us a **Paradox Diagnosis (Reify!** can always produce new sets), (iii) when axiomatised by Lin, it **Interprets** a good theory of sets (namely ZFC), and (iv) we have a **Capture**-theorem; ZFC allows you to find a Kripke model for Lin and ZFC proves that every set lives in said model. For these reasons, I think it's fair to say that the strong iterative conception is a very satisfying conception of set. Modal set theory, suitably formulated, pushes the idea that ZFC should be true of the sets, and if ZFC is adopted, we can show that a sensible modal theory is a *mathematical fact of life* – if you have ZFC you also have the strong iterative conception and all the sets live within some stage/world so described.

Whilst I don't want to deny how *good* a conception of sets the strong iterative conception of set is, I do want to press the point that it might not be the

---

68   Of course, as I've set things up here, the model in question (gotten from all the V_α) is proper-class-sized, so not a 'model' in the ordinary sense of the term. I handle this in Barton (MSb) by restricting to arbitrary set-sized models, but let's suppress these metamathematical details here.

69   See Button (2021b) for some examination of the extent to which there are definable formal relationships between modal theories of the strong iterative conception and non-modal set theory.

only option out there. Later, we'll see some examples of the weak iterative conception of set that I think are also in the running. In order to see their appeal though, we'll have to learn a little about how one can use *forcing* to build more sets.

6 Forcing as a Construction Method

In this section I want to outline forcing in set theory; a way of adding *subsets* to models. Thorough presentations are available in a wide variety of mathematical texts and full detail would just bog down the reader in an Element like this one, so my focus is on giving the informal ideas.

There's two main reasons to go into depth on this topic. First, we'll use forcing to articulate the further versions of the weak iterative conception that we'll consider later. Second, forcing is tremendously important for understanding much of the contemporary literature on the philosophy of set theory and the intuitions that underlie much work in this field. So, having a good grasp of it is no bad thing.

6.1 Forcing: The Rough Idea

A helpful way to understand forcing is by analogy with *field extensions*. Consider the relationship between the fields of real numbers $\mathbb{R}$ and complex numbers $\mathbb{C}$. One way of thinking of obtaining $\mathbb{C}$ from $\mathbb{R}$ is via the idea of *algebraic closure*. Intuitively speaking, we throw in solutions for $\sqrt{-1}$, and then by closing under the field operations, obtain $\mathbb{C}$.

Forcing is very similar. In fact, according to Paul Cohen (a father of the technique), this analogy was part of his discovery.[70] To see this analogy, let's start by considering the problem forcing was developed to solve. In particular, we were trying to prove that the continuum hypothesis is independent from ZFC. Since we knew that given a model M of ZFC, CH is true in the constructible universe of M (a fact proved in Gödel (1940)) one way to proceed was to find a way of making a model of $\neg$CH from one satisfying CH. (One could then infer by the Completeness Theorem that neither CH nor its negation followed from ZFC, assuming ZFC to be consistent.) Since we also knew that (again proved in Gödel (1940)) L was the smallest inner model (i.e. transitive model containing all ordinals) under inclusion, the natural idea was to break CH by *adding* sets – much like we could find a root for -1 by moving from $\mathbb{R}$ to $\mathbb{C}$. And this is just what Cohen did in Cohen (1963).

---

[70] See Cohen (1963), p. 113, and Cohen (2002), pp. 1091, 1093. Thanks to Carolin Antos for some discussion of the history here.

In order to figure out what we need to break CH, it's helpful to think about what CH and ¬CH say about sets of reals and functions. CH, recall, says that every set of reals (i.e. something with cardinality no bigger than $2^{\aleph_0}$) is either countable or the same size as $2^{\aleph_0}$. In this way, it says that there are lots of *kinds of function* compared with the *kinds of sets of reals* – every infinite set of reals has a function that either bijects it with $\aleph_0$ (the cardinality of $\mathbb{N}$) or $2^{\aleph_0}$ (the cardinality of $\mathbb{R}$). By contrast, ¬CH says that there are lots of *kinds of sets of reals* as compared with *kinds of function* – there's some infinite set of reals x for which there's no bijection between x and $\aleph_0$, but also no bijection between x and $2^{\aleph_0}$.

Let's suppose then that we're given a model M of ZFC + CH. What could we do to break CH? Well, we need to (i) *add* some set x to M, whilst (ii) making sure that we preserve the axioms of ZFC when we add x, and (iii) having a set of reals y in the new model such that there's no bijection between either y and the new set of all reals or natural numbers. This is what Cohen showed was possible with forcing. Assuming ZFC is consistent, there's a model M satisfying ZFC (by Completeness). Either (i) M satisfies ¬CH (in which case we're done) or (ii) M satisfies CH. If (ii), we can then add a bunch of reals G to M, and close under definable operations to form an extension $M[G]$ satisfying ZFC. In this new model $M[G]$, you can show that the *old* set of reals from M is a set of reals that is neither bijected with $\aleph_0$ nor $2^{\aleph_0}$ in $M[G]$.

If you haven't encountered forcing much before, I want the reader to now stop and pause to think about how, given the rough idea of forcing, we might be able to take a model of ¬CH and make CH true again by *adding sets*. What kind of set could we add to a model of ¬CH in order to restore CH again (and what would we have to simultaneously *avoid* adding)? (Bear in mind that you can't add natural numbers by forcing – a student once made the ingenious suggestion to me that we bump up the size of $\aleph_0$. Alas, this doesn't work since forcing keeps models transitive, and the natural numbers are isomorphic in all transitive models of set theory.)

The answer is that we need to add *functions* that provide the relevant bijections between the old sets of reals and either $\aleph_0$ or $2^{\aleph_0}$, and do so (i) without *adding reals*, and whilst (ii) preserving ZFC. Again, Cohen showed that forcing lets you do this. Given an M satisfying ¬CH, one can *collapse* the cardinals between $\aleph_0$ and $2^{\aleph_0}$ to $\aleph_0$ by adding a set H that allows you to get surjections from the natural numbers to these cardinals. In the new model $M[H]$, CH is true, since there are now bijections between $\aleph_0$ and the old 'cardinals' between $2^{\aleph_0}$ and $\aleph_0$ (i.e. things that were cardinals between $\aleph_0$ and $2^{\aleph_0}$ in the ground model).

These two kinds of forcing are sufficient to show the following:

Theorem 32 *Given a model M of ZFC, so long as we can do forcing over M, then M has:*

(1) *An extension M[G] such that M[G] satisfies ¬CH. This can be done using forcing that* collapses no cardinals – *it does not add new bijections that make any set look smaller than before.*

(2) *An extension M[H] such that M[H] satisfies CH. This can be done by forcing whilst* adding no new reals – *we don't add any new subsets of the natural numbers.*

In this sense CH is like a set-theoretic light switch as regards forcing – we can flip it on and off at will by successively forcing to add new sets, and all whilst preserving ZFC.[71] Indeed, forcing is *incredibly flexible*. An example that will be important for us is the following:

Theorem 33 *Assume that we can always force over M. Then for any set x in M, there is a forcing extension M[G] in which x is countable.*

As discussed earlier, the idea for proving this theorem is just to add a surjection from $\aleph_0$ to x.

Forcing thus provides us with a very controlled way of adding subsets to models. We'll discuss this a little in a ⚹-section later on (Section 6.2), but it will be helpful to indicate the shape of what is to come. Forcing, I want to contend, can be thought of as a *method of set construction* for adding subsets to a universe and in particular might be a way of generating sets under the *weak* iterative conception. Using this idea, we'll end up with the motivation of a concept of set on which every set is countable, since given a set x at some stage/world, we could always add a surjection from the natural numbers to x by forcing.

6.2 ⚹ A Little More Depth on Forcing

In this section I add a little more mathematical detail and provide an intuitive characterisation of forcing. This whole section is a ⚹-section, so the reader shouldn't get bogged down in the details unless they really want to. Still, the section will help inform the idea that we can think of forcing as a

---

[71] This terminology of 'switches' is from Hamkins and Loewe (2008).

way of constructing new sets from old, so I recommend at least giving it a go. Good introductions to this material can be found in Kunen (1980) and its update Kunen (2013) (a wonderful pair of books explaining a range of issues in detail), Drake and Singh (1996) (a nice concise introduction), and Weaver (2014) (a much easier-going introduction before the applications starting in ch. 14). Many set theory texts contain an introduction, however, and the reader should feel free to shop around.

We'll start with an example that will help us follow what comes later a bit better. We'll take the idea of *adding a Cohen real*. Let's suppose that you're in a model of ZFC. For now, we'll assume that the model is countable (and transitive) and so (by Cantor's theorem for the reals) misses out a whole bunch of real numbers. For our purposes, you can think of a real number as an infinite ω-length sequence of 0s and 1s (this, in turn, can be thought of as a function from the natural numbers into $\{0, 1\}$, which says whether there's a 0 or a 1 in the nth place). I want to now add in a new real number, and do so in such a way that ZFC is satisfied. So I slowly go through deciding on what I want in the nth place of my new real for each n (perhaps not in order). I need to do two things: (i) make sure I'm avoiding the reals of M (i.e. I don't get something I already have), and (ii) make sure that when I'm done I close under new definable operations to ensure ZFC is true. This is what forcing lets you do. Such an object (a new ω-length sequence of 0s and 1s) is our new real number (our 'Cohen real').

Let's now take a little peek into the tricky machinery of how we do this. The way I suggest thinking of forcing is as a way of talking about descriptions of collections that can change their members as we make certain decisions. In the end, if we make decisions in exactly the right way, we'll end up defining a new object that isn't currently in the universe we start in, and fill in all the needed sets to make ZFC true. The rough ingredients of forcing are the following (i) a *partial order* $\mathbb{P} = (P, <_\mathbb{P})$ with certain nice properties that make it sufficiently 'interesting'. You can think of $\mathbb{P}$ as the space of possible 'decisions' that we might take. (ii) $\mathbb{P}$-names: these are descriptions of collections that can change their membership depending on what decisions we take from $\mathbb{P}$, (iii) *dense sets*: these are like *advisors*; no matter what decisions you've taken, they'll always recommend at least one more you might go on to take, and (iv) a *generic filter*: this you can think of as a complete description of all the decisions that were taken in the limit, consistent with every recommendation given by an advisor. Let's look at these in more detail.[72]

---

[72] **Note:** Often authors (e.g. Drake and Singh (1996) and Weaver (2014)) write in information-theoretic terms, $\mathbb{P}$ is a space of *information*, and we slowly get more and more fine-grained information as we move through $\mathbb{P}$. The way I'm expressing things is essentially equivalent,

First, we need the notion of a *forcing partial order* ($\mathbb{P}, \leq_{\mathbb{P}}$). Before we give the definition, a couple of notes are in order:

- **Note 1:** We often refer to elements of the partial order as 'conditions'.
- **Note 2:** Here the partial order grows 'downwards' – the intuition being that if $p <_{\mathbb{P}} q$, you've got a smaller range of possible decisions after p as compared to q. Some people write $p >_{\mathbb{P}} q$ to indicate the same state of affairs, the intuition being that you get *more* information from p as compared to q.[73]

We now define:

Definition 34 A *forcing partial order* $\mathbb{P} = (P, \leq_{\mathbb{P}})$ is a partial order $\mathbb{P}$ such that:

(i) $\mathbb{P}$ has a maximal condition $1_{\mathbb{P}}$

(ii) $\mathbb{P}$ is *atomless* – any element of p of $\mathbb{P}$ has incompatible extensions (i.e. there's $q \leq_{\mathbb{P}} p$ and $r \leq_{\mathbb{P}} p$ such that there's no s with $s \leq_{\mathbb{P}} q$ and $s \leq_{\mathbb{P}} r$).

The way I'm going to suggest one thinks about this partial order is as an information space of *possible decisions* for settling membership facts. As we'll see, we can define a class of 'names' for possible sets (these are called $\mathbb{P}$-names). These we can think of as having their membership facts settled as we take decisions through $\mathbb{P}$. The conditions of being atomless one can think of as a condition on $\mathbb{P}$ being sufficiently *interesting* or *non-trivial* – there are always incompatible decisions one could make about where to go, and there's no part of $\mathbb{P}$ that admits of 'inevitability'.

In the specific case of adding a Cohen real, we can define the following partial order:

Definition 35 Given some model M, the forcing partial order to *add a Cohen real* has as its domain (in M) all finite partial functions from ω into $\{0, 1\}$ and $p \in P$ extends q (i.e. $p \leq_{\mathbb{P}} q$) if and only if p extends q as a function (i.e. q's domain is a proper subset of p's, and they agree on all arguments from q's domain).

---

but a bit easier to think about philosophically, and brings the 'variable set' way of thinking to the fore a little more.

[73] See Drake and Singh (1996), p. 155, Warning 8.8.2 for discussion.

This order gives us a way of thinking of settling the nth place of a new real – as we move down through $\mathbb{P}$ we settle more and more values for a new real to be defined. In the limit, we'll have settled every bit of the real.

How to get a handle on this idea of 'settling values'? For this we'll need the definition of a $\mathbb{P}$-name. The definition looks somewhat complicated, but it can be given an intuitive backing.

Definition 36 A $\mathbb{P}$-*name* is a relation τ such that $\forall \langle \sigma, p \rangle \in \tau$ ('σ is a $\mathbb{P}$-name and $p \in P$').

The definition *looks* circular, but in fact is not since the empty set is trivially a $\mathbb{P}$-name. You can think of the $\mathbb{P}$-names as relations where other $\mathbb{P}$-names are related to conditions in $\mathbb{P}$.

The intuition to have in mind is that a $\mathbb{P}$-name is the name for a possible set. Given a bunch of good 'decisions' from $\mathbb{P}$ (we'll talk about this idea of 'a bunch of good decisions' in a second; the key notion is that of a *generic filter*), we'll evaluate the $\mathbb{P}$-names to different sets in the extension. The way this works is given a $\mathbb{P}$-name σ, we're going to rule in or out other (already evaluated) $\mathbb{P}$-names in the domain of σ according to whether or not they're related to a condition in our new object. So $\mathbb{P}$-names are a kind of 'variable collections' – they can change their mind as to what they contain as we move about in $\mathbb{P}$.[74]

The next notion we need is:

Definition 37 We say that $D \subseteq \mathbb{P}$ is *dense* if and only if for every $p \in \mathbb{P}$, there is a $q \in D$ such that $q \leq_\mathbb{P} p$.

The way of thinking about a dense set D is that it's kind of like an *advisor*. No matter where you are in $\mathbb{P}$, and what decisions you've taken, D can come up with at least one decision you could take to continue.

Next we need the notion of a *generic filter*:

Definition 38 $G \subseteq \mathbb{P}$ is a *filter on* $\mathbb{P}$ if and only if:

(i) G is non-empty.
(ii) $p \in G$ and $q \geq_\mathbb{P} p$ implies that $q \in G$ (i.e. G is closed upwards).
(iii) $p \in G$ and $q \in G$ implies that there is an $r \leq_\mathbb{P} p, q$ with $r \in G$ (i.e. G brings any two elements together).

---

[74] ⚡ Interestingly the idea of 'variable collection' corresponds well to the category-theoretic approach to forcing. See the Appendix to Bell (2011).

We furthermore say that G is M-$\mathbb{P}$-*generic* (for some model M) if and only if G intersects every dense set of $\mathbb{P}$ in M. (We'll often just abbreviate this to 'generic' and let context determine the values of $\mathbb{P}$ and M.)

The way to think of such a G is that it is a kind of 'maximal' collection of 'good decisions made'. If you include a decision $p \in G$, then you've got to include any earlier decisions that could have led there, and you've also got to be able to bring together any two decisions together later (there's no including incompatible decisions allowed). You've also got to be 'good' in that you agree with every advisor (i.e. dense set) in at least one place. Part of what genericity ensures is that you genuinely add something by avoiding sets already in your starting model, but you also don't encode any 'extra' information in what you add.

We can then talk about what happens to a $\mathbb{P}$-name when presented with a generic G.

Definition 39 We evaluate $\mathbb{P}$-names by letting the value of τ under G (written '$val(\tau,G)$' or 'τ_G') be $\{val(\sigma,G) | \exists p \in G (\langle \sigma,p \rangle \in \tau)\}$.

Again, this looks complicated, but the intuition is as follows. Remember that a $\mathbb{P}$-name can be thought of as a kind of 'variable collection' or 'name for a possible set'. When we give some G to a $\mathbb{P}$-name τ, we evaluate stepwise by analysing the valuation of all the names in the domain of τ and then we add them to τ_G according to whether they're related to some $p \in G$. In particular, if σ is a $\mathbb{P}$-name in the domain of τ, then we put σ_G into τ_G if there is a $\langle \sigma,p \rangle \in \tau$ for which $p \in G$ (and do nothing otherwise). So you can think of us running through the $p \in G$ and throwing in already evaluated $\mathbb{P}$-names according to whether a name is related to some $p \in G$.

Let's return to our example of adding a Cohen real. Consider the following conditions from the poset to add a Cohen real:

- f is defined by:
  - $f(0) = 1$
  - $f(3) = 0$
- g is defined by:
  - $g(0) = 0$
  - $g(3) = 0$

Now consider the following names:

- $\tau = \emptyset$
- $\sigma = \{\langle \tau, f \rangle\}$

- $\mu = \{\langle \tau, f \rangle, \langle \sigma, g \rangle\}$
- $v = \{\langle \tau, f \rangle, \langle \tau, g \rangle, \langle \sigma, f \rangle, \langle \sigma, g \rangle, \langle \mu, f \rangle, \langle \mu, g \rangle\}$

Let's suppose that $f \in G$ but $g \notin G$. So this says that the first bit of our new real is 1, and the third bit is 0. What happens to our $\mathbb{P}$-names under G? Well, τ is trivial and so remains unchanged. We now have a value τ_G for τ, so the values σ, μ, and v will contain $\tau_G = \emptyset$ (since we have $\langle \tau, f \rangle \in \sigma, \mu, v$). The evaluation of σ is now complete, and we know that $\sigma_G = \{\emptyset\}$. For μ, since we know $g \notin G$, we *don't* throw in the evaluation of σ into μ_G, and so $\mu_G = \{\tau_G\} = \{\emptyset\}$. For v, whilst we do have a bunch of $\mathbb{P}$-names correlated with g (and so the evaluation of those names doesn't make it in via any ordered pair of the form $\langle \xi, g \rangle$), we also have that v contains $\langle \tau, f \rangle$, $\langle \sigma, f \rangle$, and $\langle \mu, f \rangle$ and so the interpretation of these names gets thrown in. So $v_G = \{\tau_G, \sigma_G, \mu_G\} = \{\emptyset, \{\emptyset\}\}$.

Of course, things are much more complicated when we move to names with more structure (in particular, once you have big infinite names, things are going to get more subtle) and start to consider further partial functions in G. The fact that $f \in G$ told us only about the values of bits in the 0th and 3rd spots. But there will be many more functions; since G has to hit *every* dense set, you can think about G as filling in more and more spaces in our real to be defined as we hit more and more dense sets, whilst preserving filter-hood. So we might also have the partial function $h \in G$ such that:

- h is defined as follows:
  - $h(0) = 1$ (note that h has to agree with f, since we assumed $f \in G$)
  - $h(1) = 1$
  - $h(2) = 1$
  - $h(3) = 0$ (again because h has to agree with f)
  - For every n such that $3 < n < 9001$, $h(n) = 0$.

This function tells us that our new real will have a 1 in the 0th place, a 1 in the 1st place, a 1 in the 2nd place, and 0s all the way up to the 9,000th place (it leaves open what happens over 9,000). Correspondingly, the evaluation of names will get quite complex as we have to evaluate across all the relevant $\mathbb{P}$-names, also bearing in mind that if $h \in G$, there must be a lot more conditions also in G (e.g. since G is a filter, f is also going to have to be in there if h is, since h extends f). Even if $h \in G$, there will always be a dense set D which doesn't contain any conditions $p \geq_{\mathbb{P}} h$, and so G will have to contain a function settling more than h does, thereby fixing the values of more $\mathbb{P}$-names, and so on. Once we've hit every dense set whilst preserving filter-hood, we'll have our generic G settling every bit of a new real, and this can be used to evaluate every $\mathbb{P}$-name, giving us our new extension $M[G]$.

These ideas are very difficult when one first encounters them, and should be paired with a text that goes through forcing in full mathematical detail. However, I hope the rough idea is clear. We have a 'space of possible decisions' (the partial order $\mathbb{P}$), a bunch of names that can change their mind about what they contain when presented with some 'decisions' from $\mathbb{P}$ (i.e. the $\mathbb{P}$-names), and a bunch of 'advisors' (the dense sets) each of which can always present to you a way of continuing after some point in $\mathbb{P}$. We're then given a 'maximal good bunch of decisions' (the generic G) that agrees with every dense set at some point and lets you find your way through $\mathbb{P}$ by giving you conditions from $\mathbb{P}$. G tells each $\mathbb{P}$-name who they are by ruling in evaluations of $\mathbb{P}$-names based on whether the names in the domain of a $\mathbb{P}$-name are related to the decisions in G.

Other partial orders that are especially important are:

Definition 40 Forcing to add κ-many Cohen reals.

- P is the collection of all finite partial functions (in M) from $\kappa \times \omega$ to $\{0, 1\}$
- $p \leq_{\mathbb{P}} q$ if and only if p extends q as a function.

A generic for this partial order doesn't just add a Cohen real and then close under definability, it adds κ-*many*. One can then show that you don't destroy any cardinals by adding a generic for $\mathbb{P}$ (this is a non-trivial lemma)[75]. This then lets you infer (picking big enough κ) that $\neg$CH holds in $M[G]$; even if M satisfies CH, all the cardinals between ω and κ in M are now cardinalities between ω and κ (which is now the cardinality of the continuum) of different sets of reals in $M[G]$.

As mentioned earlier, any cardinal can be collapsed to the countable using forcing. This is done using:

Definition 41 The forcing to *collapse κ to ω* is defined by:

- P is the collection of all countable partial functions from ω into κ.
- $p \leq_{\mathbb{P}} q$ if and only if p extends q as a function.

A generic for this partial order allows us to get a surjection from ω to κ, and collapses the cardinality of κ (and any sets bijective with κ) to ω.

---

[75] See, for example, Weaver (2014), p. 50, theorem 13.3.

These represent just a taste of some of the possibilities available using forcing. As Joel-David Hamkins (2012) writes (about model-building methods
including forcing):

Set theorists build models to order. (p. 417)

So forcing is a flexible tool that gives us a way of adding sets to models.
There are two points we should note. First:

Fact 42 If $\mathbb{P}$ is a forcing partial order in a model M of ZFC, and G is $\mathbb{P}$-M-
generic, then $G \notin M$. In particular, $\mathbb{P} - G = \{p | p \in \mathbb{P} \wedge p \notin G\}$ is dense (and
clearly missed by G).

This fact will be a little important later when we relate 'paradoxes'
related to forcing and the Cantor–Russell reasoning (I relegate a proof to a
footnote.[76])

Fact 43 Let M be a transitive model satisfying ZFC and let $M[G]$ be the model
obtained by evaluating all the $\mathbb{P}$-names for a forcing partial order $\mathbb{P}$ and M-$\mathbb{P}$-
generic G. Then $M[G]$ also satisfies ZFC, and in particular $M[G]$ is the smallest
transitive model of ZFC containing both every element of M and G.[77]

The strategy for proving this is to 'cook up' $\mathbb{P}$-names that you know (by the
genericity of G) will ensure that ZFC is satisfied. But the fact that you get the
smallest possible extension is important: It shows that you can think of the addition of a forcing generic G and evaluating the $\mathbb{P}$-names as throwing in G and
closing under definable operations – namely you don't get any 'extra' sets than
what is required to get ZFC by throwing in G so long as G is generic. For example, one can show that you don't add any ordinals when you force. In this way,
the $\mathbb{P}$-names and evaluation procedure conspire to make sure the construction
of $M[G]$ is very tightly controlled. This further reinforces the similarity between
forcing and more mathematically familiar constructions like obtaining the field
of complex numbers from the field of real numbers. There, we take $\mathbb{R}$, throw
in i, and close under the usual field operations to get $\mathbb{C}$. Indeed, $\mathbb{C}$ is the *smallest* such field. So with forcing, $M[G]$ is the *smallest* model of ZFC you get by
throwing in G and closing under every operation you can define.

---

[76] *Proof.* Suppose $p \in \mathbb{P}$. We must show that there is $q \in \mathbb{P} - G$ such that $q \leq_{\mathbb{P}} p$. The only non-
   trivial case is where $p \in G$. Because $\mathbb{P}$ is non-atomic, there are incompatible r and s extending
   p. But then one of r and s isn't in G – all elements of G are compatible with one another.
[77] See Kunen (2013), lemma IV.2.19.

(1) Start with forcing partial order $\mathbb{P} \in M$

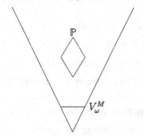

(2) Meet every dense set in M to get generic $G \subseteq \mathbb{P}$ such that $G \notin M$

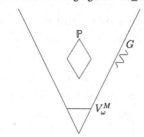

(3) Close under the evaluation of $\mathbb{P}$-names to obtain $M[G]$

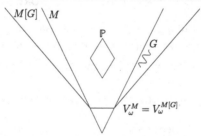

Figure 3 Forcing: (1) We start with a forcing partial order $\mathbb{P} \in M$. (2) Assuming that we can meet every dense set of $\mathbb{P}$ in M, we can get a generic $G \subseteq P$ such that $G \notin M$. Finally (3) We add G to M, and then, by evaluating the $\mathbb{P}$-names, close under definable operations to obtain the forcing extension $M[G]$.

Moreover, there's a sense in which finding such a G can be thought of as a *set-construction method* in its own way. If we're given a forcing partial order $\mathbb{P}$ and a family of dense sets $\mathcal{D}$ (let's let each dense set D_i in $\mathcal{D}$ be indexed by some i in an index set I), we can think of successively hitting each D_i in such a way that we extend our previous choices. In particular, if we start with some M and $\mathcal{D}$ is the collection of *all* dense sets available in M, what we obtain in the limit (hitting each D_i) will be an M-generic filter G. It's a substantive assumption to assume that this can always be done, but not one without intuitive pull. And if we can always perform this action for any given $\mathbb{P}$ and $\mathcal{D}$, then we can always force. We can see a visualisation of this idea in Figure 3.

6.3 Philosophical Upshot

I hope that the reader finds the preceding discussion helpful, and in particular it can serve as a road-map if you want to learn forcing in detail (alongside an introductory text). However, it's understandable if readers newer to set theory didn't pick up everything. I therefore want to quickly identify the following:

Main Philosophical Upshot You can think of moving from M to $M[G]$ by forcing as a way of *constructing new sets*.

Before we move on, we should note that this is a somewhat controversial claim. Brauer (MS), for example, raises some queries about whether one can really think of forcing as a way of generating new sets. I hope I've addressed these worries here (I argue this case further in Barton (MSb)). For now, I'm happy to take the **Main Philosophical Upshot** as an assumption from hereon out, but we will raise some open questions about it in Section 10.

7 A 'New' Kind of Paradox?

In this chapter I want to argue that there's a tension at the heart of set theory. We'll then (Section 8) explain how this can be resolved into different conceptions, much as we saw with the naive conception of set.

7.1 The Forcing-Saturated Strong Iterative Conception of Set

A popular thought in set theory is that *richness* is an essential part of set theory; there should be as many sets as possible.[78] Given this thought, it's natural to want the universe to be closed under lots of different kinds of set-construction method. Since we just saw that forcing is one such method, and we already know that the strong iterative conception is a good conception of sets, the looks attractive:

Definition 44 (Informal) The *forcing-saturated strong iterative conception of set* holds that new sets are formed from old by either (i) forming each possible plurality of sets over that stage into a set, or (ii) adding in a generic for a partial order and a family of dense sets.

So, we have two main set-construction methods (plus union, which allows us to bundle limit stages together). We can either add in a forcing generic, or we can form the powerset of a set. Clearly then, we have:

---

[78] See Incurvati (2017) for a survey of this idea in set theory.

Powerset The Powerset Axiom holds.

We're going to shortly see some conflicts with **Powerset**. We therefore define:

Definition 45 ZFC with the Powerset Axiom removed will be called ZFC⁻.

> ℞ **Note:** Dropping the Powerset Axiom is a slightly subtle business. When we formulate ZFC solely with Replacement (and treat Separation and Collection as theorem schemas), then deleting the Powerset Axiom results in a theory weaker than one would like (the version with Separation and Collection has more consequences than with Replacement alone). Since we included Separation and Collection as separate axiom schemas when formulating ZFC earlier, we avoid this complication. See Zarach (1996) and Gitman et al. (2016) for discussion.

Since we can also introduce a generic for any forcing partial order and family of dense sets under the forcing-saturated strong iterative conception, we'll introduce the following axiom:

Definition 46 (ZFC⁻) The *Forcing Saturation Axiom* or FSA is the claim that for *any* partial order $\mathbb{P}$ and set $\mathcal{D}$ consisting solely of dense sets for $\mathbb{P}$, there is a generic G intersecting every member of $\mathcal{D}$.[79]

The forcing saturated strong iterative conception then motivates:

Forcing Saturation The Forcing Saturation Axiom holds.

Readers familiar with forcing may already see the problem with the forcing-saturated strong iterative conception. For the reader that doesn't, I suggest briefly pausing to think about what **Powerset** entails (especially in light of Cantor's theorem) and what follows from **Forcing Saturation** (especially given collapse forcings).

7.2 The Cohen–Scott Paradox

Here's the problem: The forcing-saturated strong iterative conception motivates both **Powerset** and **Forcing Saturation**, but they're inconsistent with

---

[79] See Barton and Friedman (MS), Definition 9.

one another. This mirrors how the naive conception was brought down by **Universality** and **Indefinite Extensibility**. I'll refer to the paradox I'll give as the *Cohen–Scott Paradox* as it originates with the mathematical work of Cohen, and Scott was one of the first to propose the tension I'll identify. The paradox is thus not really that 'new', and the idea that there might be a tension between having uncountable sets and always being able to force has been around since at least the 1970s. However, recent work has developed the philosophy and mathematics of these ideas substantially.[80]

Letting "Powerset" denote the Powerset Axiom, the current theory motivated by the forcing-saturated strong iterative conception is $ZFC^- + $ Powerset $+ $ FSA. But we can now note that because we can produce a generic for any forcing partial order and family of dense sets, for any set x we like we can use collapse forcing to add a generic making x countable. In fact, we can note the following:

Fact 47 (ZFC^-) The forcing saturation axiom is equivalent (modulo ZFC^-) to the axiom "Every set is countable".[81]

We can now present the Cohen–Scott Paradox:

> **The Cohen–Scott Paradox** Simply put, $ZFC^- + $ Powerset $+ $ FSA implies that there are uncountable sets (by Cantor's theorem and the Powerset Axiom) but also that every set is countable (by the Forcing Saturation Axiom). Contradiction!

Before we continue, I want to emphasise: No reasonable classical set theorist has ever accepted both **Forcing Saturation** and **Powerset** in this generality. Perhaps someone learning forcing might unwittingly fall into the trap of accepting the forcing-saturated strong iterative conception, or perhaps it's appealing to theorists of a dialethic persuasion. But set theorists are a clever bunch, and they are able to see this contradiction coming a mile off. In fact, this tension has been noticed for a while. Discussing forcing in the introduction to Bell's book on the subject, Dana Scott (1977) writes:

> I see that there are any number of contradictory set theories, all extending the Zermelo–Fraenkel axioms: but the models are all just models of the first-order axioms, and first-order logic is weak. I still feel that it ought to be

---

[80] See, for example, Meadows (2015), Scambler (2021), Builes and Wilson (2022), and Barton and Friedman (MS). Naming the problem "The Cohen–Scott Paradox" is taken from Barton and Friedman (MS).

[81] This is a well-known folklore result, but see Fact 10 of Barton and Friedman (MS) for details.

possible to have strong axioms, which would generate these types of models as submodels of the universe, but where the universe can be thought of as something absolute. Perhaps we would be pushed in the end to say that all sets are countable (and that the continuum is not even a set) when at last all cardinals are absolutely destroyed. (p. xv)

So the Cohen–Scott 'Paradox' is certainly not new, and was noticed from the inception of forcing. One might then ask: If it's so obviously bad, why even consider the forcing-saturated strong iterative conception? The reason to do so is not that individual agents hold it, but that it forces us to face a possible *choice*. Much as we saw with the naive conception, there are different ways we could go. We could adopt a version of the logical conception that validates **Universality**. Or we could adopt a version of the combinatorial iterative conception on which **Indefinite Extensibility** holds. Similarly, we could now adopt **Powerset** (for example by holding the strong iterative conception) or we could adopt a conception that validates **Forcing Saturation**. We'll explore this in more detail shortly (in Section 8). For now I want to consider the relationship between the Cohen–Scott Paradox and diagonalisation.

7.3 ⚡ The Cohen–Scott Paradox and Diagonalisation

To see the link with 'diagonal' arguments, we start with the question:

Question. What (if any) is the link between the Cantor–Russell reasoning and the Cohen–Scott Paradox?

We have already seen a tight link between Russell's Paradox and Cantor's Paradox in Section 3 – in the case where we first take the universal set, then consider the identity surjection/injection, and then run the standard proof of Cantor's theorem, we get the Russell set.

There is a superficial similarity here, in that the (un)countability of some set x can be viewed as a claim about the (non-)existence of a surjection from ω to x. But is there any deeper similarity?

As mentioned earlier, the assumption that every set is countable (i.e. for any set x there is a surjection from ω to x) is *equivalent* (over ZFC⁻) to the claim that for any forcing partial order and any set-sized family of dense sets $\mathcal{D}$, there is a generic intersecting $\mathcal{D}$ (i.e. the Forcing Saturation Axiom).[82] We can now present the following 'diagonal' version of the Cohen–Scott Paradox.

---

[82] (⚡) See Barton and Friedman (MS), Fact 16.

The Cohen–Scott Paradox, Diagonal Version. If the Powerset Axiom is true, then the family $\mathcal{D}^*$ of *all* dense sets for a forcing partial order $\mathbb{P}$ is a set-sized family. By the Forcing Saturation Axiom, there is a generic G intersecting every member of $\mathcal{D}^*$. Now consider $E = \{p|p \notin G\}$. It's an exercise to show that E is dense, the interested reader can go back and find the proof in Section 6. Since G is generic for $\mathcal{D}^*$ and E is dense, we know that G intersects E at some point p. But then we have $p \in G \leftrightarrow p \in E$ (by choice of p), but $p \in E \leftrightarrow p \notin G$ (by the definition of E), and so $p \in G \leftrightarrow p \notin G$ (putting together the biconditionals), contradiction![a]

---

[a] See here also Meadows (2015) for emphasis of this diagonal version of the Cohen–Scott Paradox.

The point to note here is that there is a similarity to the Cantor–Russell reasoning. There we had the assumption of the existence of a particular surjection leading to contradictory claims about (non-)self-membership. Here we have the existence of an surjection, whilst not leading to contradictory claims about *self*-membership, we do have the contradictory $p \in G \leftrightarrow p \notin G$. So whilst the analogy is not perfect, we have a diagonal-style contradiction obtained by assuming the existence of a particular surjection. We'll discuss a possible significance of this in Section 10.4.

7.4 Summing Up

To sum up, we've seen that:

(1) There is a tension between **Forcing Saturation** and **Powerset**.
(2) This can be put in terms of a diagonal argument, with similarities to the Cantor–Russell reasoning.

So, what to do about this state of affairs?

8 Countabilist Conceptions of Iterative Set

We've identified a tension between **Forcing Saturation** and **Powerset**, in analogy with **Universality** and **Indefinite Extensibility**. And just as before, we can move forward by dropping one of the two. One way is to just hold that **Forcing Saturation** should be dropped and **Powerset** accepted. The result of doing so is the strong iterative conception, and is perhaps the 'default' position. We can then (as noted in Section 5) provide a *modal* theory of this conception using Lin (perhaps with some resources added to guarantee that we really do get all pluralities formed as sets at every subsequent world). This yields the extreme form of uncountabilism that is standardly associated with set theory with an unending hierarchy of uncountable cardinals. But might there be a way of going forward with **Forcing Saturation** instead of **Powerset**? In this section we'll see some modal theories that validate **Forcing Saturation**. Later (Section 9) we'll discuss how these conceptions interpret mathematics, and compare the two approaches in light of the theoretical virtues adumbrated in Sections 2, 4, and 5.

8.1 Countabilist Stage Theories

As we've seen, if you're going to have **Forcing Saturation**, then every set is going to be countable. For the sake of brevity, it will be helpful to introduce some terminology:

Definition 48 The *countabilist axiom* (or Count) is the axiom 'Every set is countable'.

Definition 49 (Informal) We will refer to the view that holds Count as *countabilism* (with *countabilist* the corresponding adjective), and *uncountabilism* as the position that there are uncountable sets.

It's fair to say that countabilist options for the (weak) iterative conception have been a lot less studied than the 'standard' strong iterative conception, and so we will have to proceed with a little more care in articulating the alternative. This way of viewing the sets is still somewhat nascent with much work still to be done, and we will have to be cautious in our conclusions. Certainly it is less solidified than the standard strong iterative conception, and I don't want to overstate my case. I *do* want to identify, however, that it's an *attractive* alternative. This section, then, will have the flavour of explaining a *promising road of inquiry*, rather than the more established picture of the strong iterative conception we saw in Section 5.

Since we have Count for the countabilist, we can't have uncountable sets. For this reason, we're going to have to drop the Powerset Axiom and adopt $ZFC^- + Count$. Since we don't have the Powerset Axiom (indeed we have its negation) we don't have the V_α, and so we're going to have to adopt the weak iterative conception, rather than the strong iterative conception. So the question then becomes: Given that the V_α are out, what could our stages/worlds be, and how are they constructed? Recall that for any weak iterative conception we need:

    (i) A description of what counts as a starting domain.
    (ii) A description of some methods for forming new sets from old.

Can we come up with weakly iterative theories for the countabilist, and thereby give a story along the lines of (i) and (ii)? And, in particular, is there a modal theory of sets that can function for the countabilist much like Lin did for the uncountabilist; providing a good modal theory of set construction that upholds their view?

8.2 Reify! and Generify!

I want to argue that there are proposals in the literature that *can* be viewed as providing **Natural** modal theories for countabilist versions of the weak iterative conception.

Regarding (i): What might the *set-construction* be? Well, one possibility is familiar – given some stage/world we want a notion of forming sets out of the pluralities available at that stage (i.e. **Reify!**). This is what the Powerset Axiom codifies – every possible class at some stage V_α is reified into a set (if it didn't already exist) at $V_{\alpha+1}$ (this can be partially formalised modally by Lin, and by using bimodal operators guaranteed). But note, we don't have to turn *every possible class* in a set at a subsequent stage. This is made clear by the constructibilist conception and the constructible hierarchy, at $L_{\alpha+1}$ we reify those classes *definable* over L_α into sets. In this sense, taking the definable powerset is a kind of **Reify!** set-construction method, but it's not the maximal such (that would be powerset). For example, in the L_α-hierarchy we'll get the 'universal plurality' of the previous stage at the next one, since $x = x$ is a perfectly good formula. To be a **Reify!** command you only need take *some* possible pluralities of the domain and reify them into sets; you don't have to take *all* possible pluralities.

However, as I hope I convinced the reader in Section 6, another kind of set-construction method is *forcing*. We can thus think of having, in addition to whatever **Reify!** commands we employ, a class of **Generify!** commands which will take in a partial order $\mathbb{P}$ and family $\mathcal{D}$ of dense sets and spit out a generic for $\mathbb{P}$ and $\mathcal{D}$. Closely linked is the set-construction method I'll call **Enumerate!**; this adds an enumeration between a set and the natural numbers. There are a class of **Enumerate!** commands that can be thought of as special cases of the **Generify!** operation, in particular the specific case of the forcing that adds a surjection from the natural numbers to a set.[83] If we think that the stages should support **Generify!**, then **Enumerate!** will always be executable. This idea has

---

[83] There might be other **Enumerate!** commands. A set being generic entails that you don't add in 'extra information', and an arbitrary enumeration might add in much more. For example, $0^\sharp$ can be thought of as a particular kind of countable set (and hence an enumeration), but can't be added by standard forcing techniques. See Barton (MSb) for discussion.

been advocated recently by a few authors. For example, Chris Scambler (2021) writes:

> The guiding idea . . . is to introduce another way of extending a given universe of sets as an option at each stage of the process. Specifically, we will imagine we are capable not only of introducing sets whose members are among already given things..., but also of introducing new functions between already given (infinite) sets, and in particular of introducing functions defined on the natural numbers and whose range contains any set as a subset. (p. 1088)

Jessica Wilson and David Builes (2022) express a similar idea (partly drawing on Scambler (2021)):

> Recall that any set-theoretic universe is ultimately generated by two sorts of processes: the powerset operation and the length of the ordinals. Proponents of height potentialism maintain that the length of the ordinals is indefinitely extensible: necessarily, for any ordinals, there could always be more. The modal approach to [Cantor's theorem] simply extends this line of thought to the powerset operation: necessarily, for any subsets of an infinite set, there could always be more. This is width potentialism. For any set-theoretic structure, there is both a taller one and a wider one. (p. 2212)

Recall how we could use **Even!** and **Odd!** to obtain the hereditarily finite sets. Can we think of interleaving **Reify!** and **Generify!** to obtain a modal theory for countabilist set theories? The answer is yes.

8.3 ✵ A Reifying and Generifying Modal Theory

Scambler (2021) has provided a modal theory of sets that can be used for countabilist versions of the weak iterative conception. He starts with the background of $\mathscr{L}_{<,\in}^{\diamond}$ but adds two modal operators $\langle v \rangle$ (for 'vertical' modality – reifying the pluralities of the model into sets) and $\langle h \rangle$ (for 'horizontal' modality – adding in subsets via forcing). Call this language $\mathscr{L}_{\in,<}^{\diamond,\langle h \rangle,\langle v \rangle}$. Boxes $[h]\phi$ and $[v]\phi$ are defined as $\neg\langle h \rangle\neg\phi$ and $\neg\langle v \rangle\neg\phi$ as usual. In this context, the general $\diamond$ can be thought of as 'possible through some combination of $\langle v \rangle$ and $\langle h \rangle$'.

Scambler then provides the following axioms:[84]

Definition 50 Sca consists of the following axioms in $\mathscr{L}_{\in,<}^{\diamond,\langle h \rangle,\langle v \rangle}$ (again I'll focus on giving more informal statements, the reader should go to Scambler (2021) for the formal details):[85]

---

[84] See Scambler (2021), p. 1091. I'm following the presentation in Barton (MSb).

[85] Scambler uses the term "M" (for **Meadows**) to denote Sca, as he takes inspiration for his view from Meadows (2015). As we'll see later, Meadows' work (drawing on Steel (2014)) is slightly different (he considers proper class models); therefore I've chosen "Sca".

(i) Classical first-order logic.

(ii) Impredicative plural logic.

(iii) Classical S4.2 with the Converse Barcan Formula for every modality.

(iv) **Plural Membership Definiteness** (which is, recall, the scheme):

$$(\forall x \prec yy)\Box\phi(x) \rightarrow \Box(\forall x \prec yy)\phi(x)$$

(v) The necessity of distinctness and stability axioms for $\prec$ and $\in$.

(vi) **Foundation.** The Axiom of Foundation (the standard one from ZFC).

(vii) **Extensionality.** Extensionality for sets (again, no different from ZFC).

(viii) **Weakening Schemas.** $\langle h\rangle\phi \rightarrow \Diamond\phi$ and $\langle v\rangle\phi \rightarrow \Diamond\phi$, for every ϕ.

(ix) **Vertical Collapse.** $\langle v\rangle\exists y\Box\forall z(z \in y \leftrightarrow z \prec xx)$.

(x) **Modal Infinity.** The axiom that there could *vertically* be some things that necessarily comprise all and only the natural numbers: $\langle v\rangle\exists xx\Box\forall y(y \prec xx \leftrightarrow$ 'y is a natural number').

(xi) **Vertical Modal Powerclass.** The axiom that it's *vertically* possible to have some things that are *vertically necessarily* all the subsets of a set: $\forall z\langle v\rangle\exists xx[v]\forall y(y \prec xx \leftrightarrow y \subseteq z)$.

(xii) **Possible Generics.** The axiom 'If $\mathbb{P}$ is a forcing partial order and *dd* is some dense sets of $\mathbb{P}$, then it's horizontally possible that there is a filter meeting each dense set that is one of the *dd*'.

(xiii) **Choice.** The plural version of the **Axiom of Choice** 'For any pairwise-disjoint non-empty sets *xx*, there are some things *yy* that comprise exactly one element from each member of the *xx*'.[86]

(xiv) **Modal Collection, Separation, and Replacement.** Namely, potentialist translations of the axiom schemas of **Collection**, **Separation**, and **Replacement** under each modality.[87]

Some of these axioms deserve a mention. The **Weakening Schemas** are meant to capture the idea that if I could get a set by either reifying pluralities into sets or forcing, then such a set is possible simpliciter. **Vertical Collapse** axiomatises the idea, as with Lin, that I could reify any plurality over a world into a set. **Possible Generics** corresponds to the idea that I could always add

---

[86] Scambler throws this in with the plural logic, but we'll keep it separate.

[87] Strictly speaking, Replacement is redundant given Separation and Collection. The reason to separate these out is that Collection and Separation are strictly stronger than Replacement when Powerset is removed (see Zarach (1996) and Gitman et al. (2016)). Scambler (2021) works only with the potentialist translations of Replacement.

a generic for any partial order. One issue then is **Vertical Modal Powerclass**: Notice that the version of powerclass – the axiom asserting that it's possible to have a world with all possible subsets of a set – is restricted to the vertical modality. This will not hold with the broader modality since one can always add subsets along the horizontal modality, and so there's *no* world containing every possible subset of an infinite set.

I think that there's a good case to be made that Sca satisfies **Naturalness**. We have a picture of how sets are formed; given some sets we can either **Reify!** pluralities into sets (the vertical modality) or **Generify!** to add forcing generics (the horizontal modality).[88]

Moreover, we again get a **Paradox Diagnosis**; since pluralities can always be reified into sets, exactly the same points about the Russell plurality (the plurality of all non-self-membered sets over a given world/stage) as in the case of Lin still apply. Moreover, there are other conditions that can be shown to not determine sets. For example, since any set can always be collapsed to the countable using **Generify!**, more sets can always be made countable, and there is no set of all countable sets. Not only does this conception reject **Universality** and accept **Indefinite Extensibility** (for resolving the standard set-theoretic paradoxes), but explains why its proponent should accept **Forcing Saturation** and reject **Powerset** too (for a resolution of the Cohen–Scott Paradox).

Regarding **Interpretation**, two theorems are especially important. First we have:

Theorem 51 *(Scambler, 2021)* Sca *interprets* ZFC$^-$ + Count *under the potentialist translation (the potentialist translation, recall, takes a formula ϕ in $\mathscr{L}_\in$ to a corresponding one in $\mathscr{L}_{\in,<}^{\Diamond,\langle h \rangle,\langle v \rangle}$ by replacing every occurrence of $\forall$ with $\Box\forall$ and every occurrence of $\exists$ with $\Diamond\exists$).*[89]

So there's a sense in which when we have the full modality, thinking of the sets as constructed in a manner consonant with Sca gets us ZFC$^-$ + Count. This is a pretty nice set theory in which one can do much of the usual constructions. However, it's at least desirable to have contexts in which ZFC is true (for interpreting the higher reaches of 'standard' set theory). For this we also have:

---

[88] I discuss the **Naturalness** of Sca (in particular going through the axioms one by one) in Barton (MSb).

[89] Scambler actually shows that Sca interprets ZFC with the Powerset axiom merely removed. However, a trivial modification (adding the modal versions of Collection and Separation instead of Replacement) to his system gets you full ZFC$^-$, so we state this stronger form of the theorem. See Barton (MSb) for details. Recent work by Scambler shows that one can get more, in particular that a regularity property for reals – the $\underline{\Pi}^1_1$-Perfect Set Property – holds under Sca. See Scambler (MS) for details.

Theorem 52 *Scambler (2021) Sca interprets ZFC when we restrict to the vertical modality (i.e. when we do the potentialist translation but replace □ and ◇ by [v] and ⟨v⟩ throughout).*

So when we restrict to the vertical modality we are able to interpret ZFC (this is basically just because the vertical modality obeys Lin). However, we have to *ignore* the horizontal modality that would allow us to collapse any given uncountable set (and hence break the Powerset Axiom in the non-modal theory).

The intuition behind Sca is thus the following. We have the vertical modality that will allow us, starting with the empty set, to obtain ZFC by successively reifying classes of worlds. However, we could, at any point, choose to introduce a generic for a given partial order and family of dense sets. And, by interleaving **Reify!** and **Generify!** we can get ZFC⁻ + Count. Note that, unlike the strong iterative conception or the constructibilist conception, the stages provided by Sca need not be well-ordered. Instead, much like **Odd!** and **Even!**, we have to think of applying **Generify!** and **Reify!** appropriately. Just as if you spin out applying one of **Odd!** or **Even!** you won't get all the hereditarily finite sets, so with **Generify!** and **Reify!**. If you head off applying **Reify!** over and over again, you'll just get ZFC. And there are lots of ways of applying **Generify!** badly too (e.g. by just adding single Cohen reals over and over again). But, if we apply **Generify!** and **Reify!** *just right*, we will get ZFC⁻ + Count.

The status of **Capture** is the one thing left outstanding for Sca. Recall that **Capture** requires us to be able to produce a Kripke model for our modal theory using the non-modal interpreted theory. Recent work by Scambler can be used to show that there is a **Capture**-theorem available for Sca.[90] Since the statement is a little more involved and there are still some questions open, I'll defer its consideration until later.

8.4 ⚡ Doing without Reify!

It's worth mentioning here that one does not *need* the vertical modality in order to get a conception of set that motivates ZFC⁻ + Count. Although his work is not intended for this purpose (his focus is more linguistic), John Steel has proposed a theory of worlds and sets that will do the job without needing a vertical modality. He proposes (in Steel, 2014) a two-sorted theory with variables for sets $x_0, x_1, \ldots$ and variables for universes $W_0, W_1, \ldots$ with the following axioms (here I follow the presentation in Maddy and Meadows (2020)):

---

[90] See Scambler (MS) for the result, and Barton (MSb) for the application to **Capture**.

Definition 53 *Steel's Multiverse Axioms* are as follows:

(i) The axiom scheme stating that if W is a world, and ϕ is an axiom of ZFC, then ϕ holds at W.

(ii) Every world is a transitive proper class.

(iii) If W is a world and $\mathbb{P}$ is a forcing partial order in W, then there is a universe W' containing a generic for W.

(iv) If U is a world, and U can be obtained by forcing over some world W, then W is also a world.

(v) **Amalgamation.** If U and W are worlds, then there are G and H that are generic over them such that $U[G] = W[H]$.

A discussion of these axioms, explicitly making the link with countabilism, is available in Meadows (2015). Steel wants to use his theory to isolate the 'forcing invariant' part of set theory, regarding some sentences (like CH) as indeterminate 'pseudo-questions' (Steel (2014), p. 154). Further analysis of Steel's project on its own terms is provided by (Maddy and Meadows (2020)). However, I think we can use Steel's multiverse axioms as inspiration for a modal theory of sets for a version of the weak iterative conception. We start with some proper class model(s) of ZFC, and our method of set-construction is *just* **Generify!**.

Formally, we can provide the following axioms:[91]

Definition 54 Barton (MSb) SteMMe (for **Steel-Maddy-Meadows**) comprises the following axioms in $\mathscr{L}_{<,\in}^{\diamond}$:

(i) Classical first-order logic.

(ii) *Predicative* plural logic.[92]

(iii) Classical S4.2 with the Converse Barcan Formula for $\diamond$.

(iv) The necessity of distinctness and stability axioms for $\in$ and $<$.

(v) **Plural Membership Definiteness** (which we repeat here for ease):

$$(\forall x < yy)\Box\phi(x) \rightarrow \Box(\forall x < yy)\phi(x)$$

(vi) **The Ordinal Definiteness Schema:** This is the schema of assertions of the form:

$$\forall x(\text{'}x \text{ is an ordinal'} \rightarrow \Box\phi(x)) \rightarrow \Box\forall y(\text{'}y \text{ is an ordinal'} \rightarrow \phi(y))$$

---

[91] For more details about SteMMe, and a comparison with Sca, see Barton (MSb).

[92] I adopt *predicative* plural logic since we will only need to talk about definable classes and it will make some of the model-theoretic analysis easier. One can modify the approach to make the underlying plural logic impredicative, if one so desires. See Barton (MSb) for discussion.

(vii) The necessitation of every axiom of first-order ZFC.

(viii) **Possible Set-Generics.** The axiom 'If $\mathbb{P}$ is a forcing partial order and $\mathcal{D}$ is a set of dense sets of $\mathbb{P}$, then it's possible that there is a filter meeting each dense set that is a member of $\mathcal{D}$'.

(ix) **Modal Separation, Replacement, and Collection.** The potentialist translations of every instance of the **Separation, Replacement**, and **Collection** schemas.[93]

Regarding **Naturalness**: The idea of the SteMMe is to take some proper-class-sized model of ZFC as our starting sets and **Generify!** as our sole way of forming new sets from old. There is no **Reify!** operation. .2 axiomatises the idea that any two possibilities can be brought together, in line with Steel's **Amalgamation** axiom. Stability axioms and **Plural Membership Definiteness** are required again to ensure that neither $\in$ nor $<$ (nor subplurality-hood) can behave badly as new sets come into existence. The **Ordinal Definiteness Schema** essentially posits the Barcan Formula for the ordinals, axiomatising the principle that the ordinals can't get longer. This captures the idea that our stages are all proper-class-sized and we add the necessitation of first-order ZFC to capture the idea that ZFC holds in each of these proper class models. **Possible Set Generics** is motivated by the idea that our set-construction method is forcing, and is the axiom corresponding to **Generify!**

Regarding **Interpretation**, we can note:

Fact 55 Barton (MSb) SteMMe interprets $\mathrm{ZFC}^- +$ Count under the potentialist translation.[94]

and:

Fact 56 Barton (MSb) SteMMe interprets the potentialist translations of the scheme asserting that every axiom of ZFC holds for the constructible sets.

So, just as in Sca, we have the nice theory $\mathrm{ZFC}^- +$ Count, and we have ZFC holding in some restricted contexts. We'll critically examine how nice this theory is (especially with respect to the goals of Section 2) in Section 9.

Concerning **Paradox Diagnosis**, we should note that, in stark contrast to both the strong iterative conception and the version of the weak iterative conception axiomatised by Sca, our worlds/stages are proper classes. There is a

---

[93] There are redundancies here, but we separate them out in order to aid philosophical discussion.

[94] You in fact get a version of the Perfect Set Property too, but I'll suppress this detail for now. See Barton (MSb).

possible puzzle here – why can't we collect together the sets from one of these proper class worlds to form a set? After all, all the members of some proper classes (e.g. the ordinals) are 'available' for collection at every world. The answer is that the collection forming operation – set forcing – does not allow them to be collected. So we still have **Paradox Diagnosis** (though one that merits some serious philosophical scrutiny).[95] Although there are worlds containing proper classes, we avoid contradiction by having a suitably 'weak' operation of set formation. This provides an explanation for the advocate of SteMMe as to why the problematic classes like the Russell plurality do not form a set, though in a manner somewhat different from Sca. We are, however, given an explanation of why **Indefinite Extensibility** holds (one can always use **Generify!** to add more sets), and which of **Forcing Saturation** and **Powerset** fails (**Forcing Saturation** holds because any set can be made countable, and **Powerset** fails because one can always use **Generify!** to add more subsets of a given set).

Discussion of **Capture** I will defer until Sections 9 and 10. Like with Sca, there is a **Capture**-theorem available, but it is somewhat more complicated and its philosophical import is still open.

8.5 Summing Up

There are many details to be ironed out with these proposals (I will discuss some in the next couple of sections). For now it suffices to note that though they are somewhat nascent, there are theories like Sca and SteMMe that provide a modal theory for the weak iterative conception that validates **Forcing Saturation** and Count. That's all well and good, but we might ask at this point: Which is better out of the strong iterative conception and the forcing-saturated weak iterative conception when we bear in mind the goals of set theory?

9 Mathematics and Philosophy under the Different Conceptions

This section will examine whether one of the strong iterative conception or the countabilist versions of the weak iterative conception is best. We'll do this by looking at how mathematics is interpreted under each conception of set, and examine each with respect to the theoretical virtues we discussed in Section 2. We'll first provide an explanation of how each handles mathematics, before contrasting them side by side with respect to our theoretical virtues.

---

[95] For example, Linnebo (2010) and Studd (2019), would not take this response to be satisfactory. They think that there are good grounds for asserting that whenever we have a plurality, we can turn it into a set, and so they won't find the picture provided by SteMMe appealing.

9.1 Mathematics under the Strong Iterative Conception

Let's first recap the situation with the strong iterative conception. As we noted in Section 2, ZFC and the strong iterative conception does an extremely good job of interpreting mathematics. A couple of extra things should be mentioned though at this point.

One core problem for the advocate of the strong iterative conception is to resolve questions about **Theory of Infinity**. For, whilst they do have ZFC, this theory tells us vanishingly little about the behaviour of infinite sets, and in particular the values of the continuum function $f(\aleph_{\alpha+1}) = 2^{\aleph_\alpha}$ or whether large cardinal axioms hold. More has to be done to substantiate new axioms for set theory, and there's a rich literature on the topic.[96]

One kind of mathematics that the advocate of the strong iterative conception has to interpret are the modal countabilist theories we've discussed here. On her view, these modal theories can be construed as about the *hereditarily countable* sets (i.e. sets built up only from countable sets – formally we say that a set is hereditarily countable if it is a countable set containing only hereditarily countable sets). In this way, the advocate of the strong iterative conception holds that theorists advocating forcing-saturated weak iterative conceptions can be interpreted as talking about structures that miss out a great many *large sets* (and in particular all the uncountable ones).

9.2 Mathematics under Our Countabilist Conceptions

Things are a little more challenging under the forcing-saturated weak iterative conceptions. Because we don't have **Powerset**, we can't just piggy-back off the 'standard' account of mathematics available under the strong iterative conception.

We've seen two versions of the weak iterative conception (given by SteMMe and Sca) that validate **Forcing Saturation**. However, in this context we don't have the Powerset Axiom, and hence can't build many of the usual representations of structures that we want. So there's a number of questions we can ask about the forcing-saturated countabilist interpretation of mathematics:

(1) How should we understand the study of theories based on ZFC?
(2) What does 'mainstream' mathematics look like under this conception?
(3) What does our **Theory of Infinity** look like?

---

[96] See, for example, Maddy (1988a), Maddy (1988b), Koellner (2014), and Incurvati (2017) among many others.

9.2.1 How Should We Understand the Study of Theories Based on ZFC?

The quick answer is that you can still have ZFC *in a restricted domain*; you just can't have *all subsets* of the sets in those domains (since for any set x, there's a collapsing function from x to ω). If you want to have 'uncountable sets' you just have to leave out the subsets that witness bijections with the natural numbers.

(A parenthetical remark that should be included at this point: The idea that sets might be small but 'appear' large in some model appears in the work of Skolem, especially Skolem (1922). Often, however, Skolem's position is cashed out via a scepticism and/or referential indeterminacy by asking the question "How do I know I'm not living in/speaking about a countable model?". The present family of views does not have this flavour. It is compatible with the idea that we can refer to the universe without an issue; it is just that the level of **Forcing Saturation** is so strong that we can only talk about 'uncountable' sets by missing out functions.)

One can have very natural looking models here. For example, as well as countable transitive models, it's possible to have transitive models of ZFC containing all ordinals (so-called inner models) within a model of ZFC$^-$ + Count. Recall that, for example, Sca interprets ZFC under the vertical modality and SteMMe can get ZFC in the constructible universe. So any countabilist theory based on Sca or SteMMe has inner models of ZFC.

Aside from the use of the modal theories presented here, there are also natural axioms that get us inner models for ZFC plus large cardinals. Since the axioms are somewhat complex, I'll provide them in a ✶-box:

✶ I'll mention some in passing, but I won't go into details since the mathematics starts to get tricky. The interested reader is directed to Scambler (MS), Barton (MSb), and Barton and Friedman (MS) for further references and a fuller discussion of these examples. One way is to assert the existence of 'sharps' – these imply that there are self-embeddings from many inner models and can be used to get ZFC plus large cardinals in inner models within ZFC$^-$ + Count.[a] Another (related) kind are *regularity properties* for sets of reals. In fact, both Sca and SteMMe can interpret a scheme corresponding to a version of the perfect set property (for the cognoscenti, the Π^1_1-Perfect Set Property) which implies that there are many inner models of ZFC.[b] Other regularity properties for sets of reals (e.g. Projective Determinacy) can be (schematically) rendered in ZFC$^-$ + Count, and also imply that there are inner models of ZFC plus many large cardinals. Finally in Barton and Friedman (MS) we propose an axiom (the

Ordinal Inner Model Hypothesis), which implies that every set is count-able but also that ZFC with large cardinals added holds in inner models (again for the cognoscenti – one can get $0^{\#}$).

---

[a] See Regula Krapf's PhD thesis (Krapf (2017)) for details of handling sharps in the countabilist context.

[b] See Scambler (MS) and Barton (MSb). Defining the Π_1^1-Perfect Set Property would take us too far afield; see, for example, Kanamori (2009) (sections 11-12) for details.

There is thus a kind of 'symmetry' between the strong iterative concep-tion and the forcing-saturated weak iterative conception. Under the forcing-saturated weak iterative conception, the theories motivated by the strong iterative conception should be understood as holding in transitive models that *miss out subsets* (in particular all the collapsing functions). But under the strong iterative conception, the theories motivated by the forcing-saturated weak iter-ative conception seem to *miss out large sets* (in particular all the uncountable ones).[97]

9.2.2 Mathematics for the Countabilist

The picture of mainstream mathematics is much different when we have **Forcing Saturation**. Whilst arithmetic remains unchanged (one can have V_ω exactly as under the strong iterative conception), there are no uncountable set-sized structures. Rather, *all uncountable collections are proper-class-sized*. The study of *all the real numbers* thus becomes the study of a large proper class.[98] Since there are exactly continuum-many continuous functions between the reals, we can also think of the study of all continuous functions $f: \mathbb{R} \to \mathbb{R}$ as examining a proper class. But whilst the real numbers and class of all continu-ous functions are proper classes, yet higher mathematics for larger uncountable cardinals cannot be interpreted as about the sets without the use of even higher-order logic. For example, the classical study of the space of *all* functions $f: \mathbb{R} \to \mathbb{R}$ (a key structure for functional analysis) cannot be interpreted even by a proper class. One might ask oneself at this point whether this is *bad* or just *merely different*. We'll return to this issue later on (Section 9.3).

---

[97] In Barton (MSa) I've argued that this symmetry can be used to claim that *un*countabilism is in fact *restrictive*.

[98] In fact, since you can think of a real number as coding a countable set, the study of set theory is in a way just the study of real numbers under ZFC⁻ + Count. This is supported by the fact that second-order arithmetic and ZFC⁻ + Count are bi-interpretable. See section 5.1 of Regula Krapf's PhD thesis (Krapf (2017)) for a nice presentation of this result.

9.2.3 What Does Our Theory of Infinity Look Like?

How is **Theory of Infinity** handled? There are (at least) two different kinds of question one could ask:

(1) How should we understand the **Theory of Infinity** provided by ZFC?
(2) What is the **Theory of Infinity** simpliciter?

The former question is easily handled under the forcing-saturated weak itera- tive conception. Since ZFC is only true *relative to a model* that misses out sets, the behaviour of the continuum function (as well as other independent sen- tences) should be understood via the diverse world-to-world information we get out of the different models of ZFC. This has affinities with some so-called multiverse views in the philosophy of set theory (we'll discuss these later in Section 10; for our purposes now one can simply read 'multiverse' as the col- lection of all countabilist worlds). For example, Joel-David Hamkins (2012) writes:

> the continuum hypothesis is a settled question; it is incorrect to describe the CH as an open problem. The answer to CH consists of the expansive, detailed knowledge set theorists have gained about the extent to which it holds and fails in the multiverse, about how to achieve it or its negation in combination with other diverse set-theoretic properties. (p. 429)

Since there is no maximal ZFC structure for the forcing-saturated weak iter- ative conception, we have an answer to the question of CH in ZFC-based set theory. Simply put, it is to be found in how CH behaves across structures that satisfy ZFC. No further answer is needed or possible.

This answer only concerns the impoverished ZFC models for the count- abilist. So what is their **Theory of Infinity** simpliciter? This question is answered for *sets* – every set is either finite or countably infinite. So, in a sense, the countabilist has a comprehensive (albeit slightly boring) answer for the rel- ative sizes of *sets*. However, there are still some interesting questions to be had. Since the continuum is a proper class, CH is now a claim about what *proper classes* exist coding bijections between *classes* of sets and the universe. Is every infinite *class* of reals either countable or the size of the universe? This is the open question that the countabilist must address.

⚡ One very interesting fact is that in this context CH is *equivalent* to the claim that the universe is bijectable with the ordinals. So we have an immediate link with CH and versions of Global Choice. Moreover, CH is equivalent for the countabilist to the 'limitation of size' principle that all proper classes are the same size.[a] *If* the advocate of the forcing-saturated weak iterative conception could motivate this limitation of size principle, they would then have a complete story for **Theory of Infinity**. Simply put, every collection would be either (a) finite, (b) infinite, or (c) proper-class-sized, and the continuum hypothesis (rendered as a claim about proper classes) would be true.

---

[a] See Holmes et al. (2012), section 3.4.

9.3 Contrasting the Conceptions

Is one of the two conceptions better? Both have different ways of responding to **Theory of Infinity** and advocate apparently distinct pictures of the foundations of mathematics. And both have some open questions that remain outstanding.

This all raises the issue of what will become of the different conceptions, especially when we bear in mind the criteria outlined in Section 2. I won't come down one way or the other here – I think there are many questions that should be left open for the future. The main point I want to press is the following: Both are *attractive* conceptions of set.

I do think it's pretty clear that the strong iterative conception, with the rich understanding we have of it and theories motivated on its basis, is well in the lead in the race. This is to be expected; we've only recently started looking seriously at the forcing-saturated weak iterative conception, and so the strong iterative conception had an enormous head start (a good 50 years or so). Races that seemed one-sided can get more competitive over time though. For example, the logical conception is experiencing something of a resurgence due to its possible application in formal semantics having previously been regarded as almost dead in the water (or at least deeply problematic).[99] So it's worth thinking of how each responds to the desiderata outlined in Section 2, contrasting the two, and considering whether the forcing-saturated weak iterative conception might catch up. For the sake of ease, we repeat our theoretical virtues here:

Generous Arena Find *representatives* for our usual mathematical structures (e.g. the natural numbers, the real numbers) using our theory of sets.
Shared Standard Provide a standard of correctness for proof in mathematics.
Limits of Formalisation Set theory provides a natural place to examine the limits of our formalisation, pushing the boundaries of what might be

---

[99] See Linnebo (2006), Linnebo and Shapiro (2023), and Roberts (MSa).

realistically expected to be captured, and exploring where formalisations may finally give out.

Testing Ground for Paradox Set theory is very *paradox* prone, both in terms of the principles that can be formulated within set theory and when combined with certain philosophical ideas (e.g. absolute generality and mereology). In this way, set theory provides a *testing ground* for seeing when and how ideas are inconsistent.

Metamathematical Corral Provide a theory in which metamathematical investigations of relative provability and consistency strengths can be conducted.

Risk Assessment Provide a degree of confidence in theories commensurate with their consistency strength.

We also added (on conceptions of set):

Naturalness Provide a reasonably natural account of what the sets are like, one which avoids ad hoc restrictions.

Interpretation A conception should motivate a good theory of sets.

Paradox Diagnosis Respond to the explanatory challenge: Explain why the paradoxical collections aren't sets and which conditions do (and do not) determine sets.

Capture Let $T^\diamond$ be a modal theory of sets interpreting a non-modal theory T via the potentialist translation. Then we say that $T^\diamond$ satisfies **Capture** if and only if, given a model M of T, we have a general way of extracting a Kripke frame $K_{T^\diamond}^M \models T^\diamond$ from M such that for every $x \in M$ there is a world $W \in K_{T^\diamond}^M$ such that $x \in W$.

Generous arena is handled very differently by the two approaches. But each has its own answer. The strong iterative conception can essentially piggy-back off the standard account of **Generous Arena** given in Section 2. Little more needs to be said here.

The case of the forcing saturated weak iterative conception is more controversial. Here the reals are a *proper class* (at least in the non-modal theory). Set theory here is directly akin to second-order arithmetic, and analysis can be thereby interpreted (so long as we allow talk of proper classes). But third-order arithmetic is out of reach, standardly interpreted. However, since we have ZFC plus large cardinals in inner models, proofs using resources from third-order arithmetic and above can be interpreted in *restricted contexts*. Whether this constitutes a hobbling of mathematical practice or just a different approach is a question I leave open for philosophical examination.[100]

---

[100] See, for example, the debate between Solomon Feferman and John Steel in Feferman et al. (2000), as well as Tatiana Arrigoni and Sy-David Friedman's take on the matter in Arrigoni

This has implications for **Shared Standard**. Both the strong iterative conception and forcing-saturated weak iterative conception provide their own **Generous Arena**, and hence their own account of when a proof is legitimate. Each standard is very different, though, if we have **Forcing Saturation**, third-order resources are not legitimate for reasoning about the reals. So both have an account of **Shared Standard**, but the forcing-saturated weak iterative conception deviates substantially from the currently accepted norm. This said, under this countabilist approach, proofs in third-order arithmetic and/or ZFC are not *wrong*, they just need to be interpreted in *restricted contexts*. Again, I leave it open whether or not this should count *against* the position or it is simply merely *different*.

Regarding the **Limits of Formalisation**, both are able to handle Gödelian incompleteness in much the same way (claims about relative provability can be construed as claims about first-order arithmetic, and the first-order arithmetic provided by the two conceptions are not significantly different)[101]. However, since both provide very different pictures of the role of the continuum and independence, they provide quite different answers to the question of our knowledge of the continuum. The strong iterative conception has several questions to answer about large cardinal independence and the behaviour of the continuum function. The forcing-saturated version of the weak iterative conception, on the other hand, answers basically all questions about *sets*. Every set is countable, and there are *no* large (or even uncountable) cardinals, even if there are large cardinals and uncountable cardinals in inner models. Since all sets are countable, it's perhaps somewhat unsurprising that we can answer questions about them more easily. Still, the continuum hypothesis is pushed to a question about class theory, and in particular is connected with global well-orders for the universe (whether there's a proper-class-sized bijection $F: V \rightarrowtail\!\!\!\rightarrow Ord$). As we noted earlier, if such a countabilist can motivate the claim that all proper classes are the same size, then CH is solved too. But perhaps one can argue that whilst the sets are relatively easily known, the continuum/proper classes are not, and so we leave this question open. But there are at least *avenues* for making philosophical progress on this question.

---

and Friedman (2013). Relevant here is the aforementioned multiverse view provided by John Steel (in Steel (2014)) with subsequent development by Penelope Maddy and Toby Meadows (Maddy and Meadows (2020)). See also Barton and Friedman (MS) (for an argument that many of the usual foundational roles for large cardinals can be performed in the countabilist setting).

[101] Really, all one gets is that the different theories proposed will yield more/less information about the natural numbers. But any theory of arithmetic compatible with one conception is compatible with the other.

Moreover, both provide interesting perspectives as a **Testing Ground for Paradox**. This is in two ways. First, the incompatibility between **Powerset** and **Forcing Saturation** and the two conceptions we've discussed provides for an interesting kind of 'paradox' in its own right (this is part of what was at play in the Cohen–Scott Paradox). Interestingly, although each denies the full generality of the other's principles, one can incorporate *partial amounts* thereof. The proponent of **Powerset** can add in limited amounts of **Forcing Saturation**, for restricted kinds of partial order and families of dense sets (this yields a class of axioms known as *forcing axioms*). Interestingly, the addition of such restricted **Forcing Saturation** into the strong iterative conception tends to yield a resolution of CH in the negative, with $2^{\aleph_0} = \aleph_2$.[102] It is not known how to generalise these axioms for higher values of the continuum function. For the proponent of the forcing-saturated weak iterative conception of set, we can begin by noting that axioms postulating the existence of uncountable cardinals are a bit like large cardinal axioms – they (incorrectly!) assert the existence of sets closed under various kinds of operation. For example, the least uncountable cardinal can be thought of as a set that is closed under the formation of hereditarily countable cardinals. Over ZFC^-, an uncountable cardinal behaves a bit like an inaccessible cardinal does in ZFC.

🕭 For example, let κ be the least inaccessible and ω_1 be the least uncountable cardinal. Both are regular, and both provide a natural model for the base theory – V_κ provides a model for ZFC (in fact, *second-order* ZFC), and $H(\omega_1)$ provides a model for ZFC^-.

Moreover, one *can* postulate the existence of sets with closure under countabilism (just not enough to get you an uncountable cardinal). Here's a slightly tricky example:

🕭 Consider the following schematic reflection principle (for any ϕ in the language of set theory):

$$\forall x \exists a(x \in a \land \text{'}a \text{ is transitive'} \land \phi \leftrightarrow \phi^a)$$

that is, for any set x there is a transitive set a such that $x \in a$ and ϕ is absolute between a and the universe. ZFC^- with this added is known as ZFC^-_{Ref}. This theory is very weak – still far below the consistency strength of ZFC (and so is consistent if ZFC is). But it adds in sets with *closure*;

---

[102] For example, the *Proper Forcing Axiom* implies that $2^{\aleph_0} = \aleph_2$. For a survey of the Proper Forcing Axiom, see Moore (2010).

in particular, if ϕ holds in the universe, then ϕ holds restricted to some transitive set a. And since the universe exhibits various closure properties, this version of reflection will imply that there are sets with those closure properties too.

So whilst we know that we'll have to get rid of one of **Forcing Saturation** or **Powerset**, whichever way we go, we can add back in *some restricted versions* of whatever we rejected.

Metamathematical Corral can be dealt with immediately. Both conceptions motivate theories that can handle talk of set-theoretic models easily, and so there is no particular difference here. Similarly for **Risk Assessment**, whilst there might be small fluctuations dependent upon which theory is eventually picked, both conceptions can motivate theories with a good deal of strength on an independently plausible conception. We also might think that there's no need to settle on a single conception for **Risk Assessment**; so long as the conceptions seem cogent and coherent, we can have confidence in the consistency of theories that are proved consistent on each picture. In particular, if a theory U is proved consistent by theories motivated under each conception, then more power to U – its consistency is converged upon by two distinct cogent conceptions of set.

Each of **Naturalness**, **Interpretation**, and **Paradox Diagnosis** has been discussed earlier, and so I won't repeat myself. Suffice it to say, all of Lin, Sca, and SteMMe perform fine with respect to these desiderata. However, we owe the reader an explanation of **Capture**. The strong iterative conception and Lin performs perfectly here; one can use the V_α to quickly provide a Kripke model for Lin, and then (using the theorem that every set belongs to some V_α) get the result that every set lives there. For the countabilist versions of the weak iterative conception, there are **Capture**-theorems available, but since the details are a little fiddly, I relegate their discussion to a $\overset{\star}{\pi}$-box (even then though, giving all the gory details would get us too deep in the weeds, so I direct the interested reader to the relevant papers). The core point is that though one can get a **Capture**-theorem for these theories, it is still somewhat unsatisfying.

$\overset{\star}{\pi}$ The core observation used to get **Capture**-theorems for Sca and SteMMe is that both are able to interpret the schemas corresponding to a regularity property known as the $\underline{\Pi}^1_1$-Perfect Set Property (I won't define it here; many introductory texts on descriptive set theory contain the details).[a] Scambler (MS) provides the result for Sca, and Scambler's strategy can be used for SteMMe too (see Barton (MSb)). This, in turn implies that there are many inner models of ZFC (in fact, the $\underset{\sim}{\Pi}^1_1$-Perfect Set Property implies that $L[x]$ satisfies ZFC for every real x; see Solovay (1974) and Taranovsky (2004)). This regularity property can then be used to get Kripke models for Sca and SteMMe containing every set (basically using the various $L[x]$).

The slight dissatisfaction results from the fact that in the case of Lin, the Kripke model we obtain meshes very nicely with the informal description of the way sets are formed (namely via powerset and union). Indeed, the accessibility relation we get out of the V_α exactly matches some application of powerset and union-bundling. However, for the cases of Sca and SteMMe, there may be countable sets that are in the Kripke model that are not added by forcing. One might find this slightly dissatisfying – after all, aren't the modal theories supposed to be telling us how the sets are formed? Coming up with a modal theory that better meshes with the informal set-construction methods represents an open question for the advocate of forcing-saturated versions of the weak iterative conception that we'll explicitly identify in Section 10.

---

[a] See, for example, Kanamori (2009), esp. sections 11–12.

For these reasons I think that both the strong iterative conception and the forcing-saturated weak iterative conception are each viable conceptions of set. The strong iterative conception clearly fits better with current orthodoxy, but that's not a good reason to discount the forcing-saturated weak iterative conception out of hand. In the end, I think that a careful analysis is needed, either to choose one of the two or to learn to live with the pluralism they offer. For this to be done successfully, more development of these two (and other) conceptions is required, especially on the side of the juvenile weak iterative conception.

10 Conclusions, Open Questions, and the Future

A short summary of what I've argued in this Element: I think that set theory provides an interesting case study and tool for both philosophers and mathematicians. I think that progress in set theory often involves trading off different principles (e.g. **Universality** and **Indefinite Extensibility**, **Powerset** and **Forcing Saturation**). I think that this is the situation we find ourselves in now (at least to some degree).

This said, there's a *lot* more research to be done in this direction. Some areas I have already identified, but some are new and so I want to close with a summary and consolidation of what I take to be the most interesting questions for moving forward. Importantly, we'll also be able to identify further connections with philosophy more broadly (e.g. absolute generality and modal metaphysics). It will also be helpful to present some objections to what I've argued, and mention how they could be answered. This will make this 'conclusion' longer than usual, and I hope the reader will indulge me in this.

10.1 Capturing the Sets

We finished the previous section by identifying a major issue for countabilist versions of the weak iterative conception, namely the status of **Capture**. Whilst **Capture**-theorems are available, there is much work to be done here, in particular finding a conception, modal theory, and **Capture**-theorem on which the informal description of the set-construction methods matches up with the accessibility relation on the relevant Kripke frame (as is the case with Lin and the V_α). So we simply ask:

Question Is there a reasonable presentation of a modal theory $T^\diamond$ that motivates an extension T of ZFC$^-$ + Count, but where one can (in T) recover a Kripke model of $T^\diamond$ and prove that every x is a member of some stage, *and* have the relevant accessibility relation conform to the informal description of how the sets can be constructed?

As remarked earlier (Section 9) there is some progress here, but the **Capture**-theorems for Sca and SteMMe are not as good a match as we get with Lin and the V_α. We can also ask similar questions about *non-modal* theories of the weak iterative conception. Positively resolving this question would go some way to cementing countabilist weak iterative conceptions as genuine contenders, rather than up-and-coming prospects.

10.2 The Weak Iterative Conception Needs Work

Earlier (Section 8) I remarked that the strong iterative conception is further ahead in the race as compared to other versions of the weak iterative conception (and in particular countabilist ones). I want to address some concerns one might have that these countabilist conceptions are more problematic than I'm letting on (perhaps they should not even be regarded as qualifying entrants).

There are a few reasons one could give to substantiate this claim. The strong iterative conception, one might contend, is well-developed. We have an account of what the worlds are (the V_α). By contrast, the weak iterative conception seems rather underspecified, and clearly in need of sharpening by a further conception. But what are the constraints here? What is to count as a legitimate method of set-construction? These are all left unanswered by the weak iterative conception and we might worry that the weak iterative conception is not sufficiently well-formulated to provide enough constraints.

Here's a somewhat silly example of a description of an iterative process.

Definition 57 (Informal) The *trivialising conception* of set holds that sets are formed in stages. There are just two stages. At stage 0 we have nothing. At stage 1 we perform the following operation: **Form all the sets!**. There are no other stages.

What's wrong with this as a version of the weak iterative conception? I think it's important to recall (Section 3) what we want out of a conception of set. We want a conception that satisfies **Naturalness, Interpretation, Paradox Diagnosis**, and **Capture**.

This trivialising conception does not perform well here. Whilst I'm not quite sure how to assess it for **Naturalness** (and **Capture** will likely be trivially satisfied should one be able to provide a suitable theory) it performs very poorly with respect to **Paradox Diagnosis** and **Interpretation**. It doesn't explain why paradoxical collections don't get into its second stage. We have no explanation – beyond wielding a contradiction as a Dummetian 'big stick' – of why the operation **Form all the sets!** doesn't form paradoxical ones. And it is totally uninformative about the theory we should adopt. So, yes, it is a legitimate version of the weak iterative conception. But it is also *rubbish*. We can thus safely kick it to the kerb. By contrast, the countabilist versions of the weak iterative conception, with their attendant axioms and modal theories, look promising, even if slightly less developed than the strong iterative conception.

That's not to say that there aren't some questions here that need to be answered under these countabilist conceptions. An important issue is to work out the details of the modal theories for the weak iterative conception. One of the major differences between the strong iterative conception and these is that the modal theory of the former is pretty much fully worked out (beyond **Theory of Infinity** – there will be potentialist translations of sentences independent of ZFC that are up for grabs). For the latter, things are less settled (though there are options as discussed in Section 8). I want to make a few points about moving forward with the project of isolating appropriate modal theories, and the challenges that need to be overcome.

First, I think that the weak iterative conception is *extremely broad*. This is evidenced by the fact that the trivialising weak iterative conception is a legitimate version of it, even if *terrible* as a conception of set. Moreover, there are very many disparate conceptions that also fall under this banner (e.g. the constructibilist conception and the forcing-saturated conception don't seem to have a whole lot in common beyond their weak iterativity). So I don't think we are going to get a *lot* of informativeness out of the weak iterative conception alone.

However, one thing we *do* get is the idea that there should be some sort of description of the universe as unfolding as new sets are built. And I think the following *is* true: *Legitimate ways of constructing sets should be well-founded.*

Here lies the challenge for coming up with a more detailed account of the stages and/or modal theories for the weak iterative conception: Many of the possible candidates for modal theories considered in Section 8 are *not* well-founded in the sense that the corresponding frames don't have a well-founded accessibility relation. The problem concerns forcing: It's pretty rare – though not impossible – to have forcing extensions that are minimal in any interesting sense.[103]

⚡ Here's an example: Imagine I'm adding a single Cohen real to some structure M. Given such an M, there are always non-interdefinable Cohen reals G and H, and so there is a choice to be made about which to add. So such a way of adding sets is not well-ordered (under inclusion, at least).

Nor is it well-founded under inclusion; one can get denseness in the ordering. Start by identifying that for any Cohen real G, there is a Cohen real H from which G can be defined but not vice versa. Moreover, if G is definable from H but not vice versa, there is also a Cohen real I that (i) G is definable from I, (ii) I is not definable from G, and (iii) I is definable from H. Thus, given any two single-Cohen-real forcing extensions $M[G]$ and $M[H]$ such that $M[G] \subsetneq M[H]$, there is also a dense ordering of $M[I]$ between them.

Is this a knock-down? I think not. The point I wish to make is that although *accessibility* is non-well-founded in the relevant Kripke model, the notion of a *set-construction method* might still be well-founded. One just needs it to be *indeterminate* what set gets added.

To see this, here's a simpler non-set-theoretic example. Let's suppose that we're given a finite line segment $l \subset \mathbb{R}$. Suppose further that I have a single construction method **Extend!** that allows me to extend l in a single direction. Now I could extend l to the left, or I could extend l to the right. Moreover, if I extend l left, I don't get what I get if I extend l right (let's assume that l_1 and l_2 have to comprise exactly the same points to be identical). Moreover, any time I extend l in one of the two directions to a line l', there's a dense ordering

---

[103] A good example of a partial order in which one does have an interestingly 'minimal' extension is *Sacks forcing*. See Geschke and Quickert (2004) for a survey.

of smaller lines that I could have extended to (with length greater than *l* but smaller than *l'*). But this seems to me like a perfectly fine way of constructing new lines from old. Indeed, one could formalise this modally if one so desired, and a corresponding Kripke frame could have a non-well-founded accessibility relation. But the method of *construction* isn't *non-well-founded*, it's just *indeterminate*.[104] This has been recognised since at least the time of Euclid and Aristotle (indeed, there is a more-than-superficial resemblance to Zeno's dichotomy paradox). What I suggest is that one looks at the well-founded *sub-relations* of the accessibility relation. These will correspond to ways we can legitimately construct new objects from old. For the strong iterative conception, it is just their luck that their accessibility relation is well-founded and *matches* their specification of the processes involved in their version of the weak iterative conception. But this needn't be the case. It's then open to us to say that, whilst I can force to a world (and thereby see a descending sequence in the accessibility relation), the way I *get to* any world has to be doable in a well-founded way. But this suggestion, though promising, is very far from being worked out in detail and represents a substantial open question that needs to be answered for modal theories like Sca and SteMMe. So we ask:

Question Is there an account (possibly formal) of the weak iterative conception that makes clear the notion of a *legitimate method of set construction*?

A separate question that should be addressed when developing the weak iterative conception (and one I've largely sidelined in this Element) is whether it is better to cash things out in modal or stage-theoretic terms. It is very natural, as I've done throughout this Element, to think of modal theories as implicitly giving us some notion of stage, where a stage can just be identified with a world. This move isn't clearly forced on us, however. For example, we might instead choose to formulate the notion of stage directly (as in much work in the latter half of the twentieth century).[105] So we ask:

Question How do modal theories of sets and stage theories philosophically relate to one another? Should we think of them as different ways of talking about the same subject matter?[106]

10.3 The Story Is Too Neat, and Ignores Much

Throughout this Element, I've presented the idea that we can view different attractive conceptions of set as arising out of trading off **Forcing Saturation**

---

[104] See also Barton (MSb) for this argument.
[105] See Button (2021a) for a summary of the history.
[106] I thank Davide Sutto and Chris Scambler for pressing this point.

and **Powerset**. But I want to emphasise that whilst I do think this is a fundamental tension, there are *many* more options out there, some of which are weakly iterative. What about, for instance, inner model theory and the Ultimate-L programme (Woodin, 2017)? I won't go into detail about this here, but the rough idea is to come up with an 'L-like' model that is able to give a good structure theory for V and still incorporate large cardinals ($V = L$ implies that many large cardinals don't exist). There are even iterative-style set theories on which every set has a complement (see Forster (2008) and Button (2022))! And what about the cornucopia of proposals for motivating set-theoretic axioms under the strong iterative conception (e.g. Freiling's darts, determinacy, forcing axioms, reflection principles)? Aren't I presenting an all-too-narrow view of the state of the art?

Yes! It is absolutely too narrow, and space doesn't permit me to go into the full details of every possible direction in set theory. My point here was not to propose **Powerset** and **Forcing Saturation** as *the* two possibilities for set-theoretic development (though I *do* think they might be *especially* attractive to philosophers). My focus was rather to articulate the idea that in certain contexts we can see conceptions as emerging from trading off inconsistent principles, and thereby highlight some similarities between our own predicament and that of our intellectual ancestors. In particular, I made simplifying assumptions there too – there's far more out there than the conceptions I concentrated on.

Really the space of conceptions should be far broader and the distinctions not as conceptually neat as these pages might seem to indicate. I've said little about other – possibly non-iterative – conceptions of set. We might have examined the graph conception (e.g. Incurvati (2020)). There are conceptions based on non-classical logics, such as paraconsistent (e.g. Priest (2002); Jockwich et al. (2022)) or constructivist/intuitionist approaches (e.g. Feferman (2010); Bell (2014); Scambler (2020)). Others use an idea of predicativity (e.g. Feferman and Hellman (1995); Linnebo and Shapiro (2023)). Some of these may fit into the weak iterative conception mould, but there's no *requirement* to do so.

The point is just the following: This Element isn't meant to be providing a classification for every conception of set. My point is just that by considering (i) the interrelations between different conceptions, and (ii) how we trade off inconsistent principles, we can come to understand better the space of possibilities for articulating the mathematically fertile notion of collection. There is a huge amount of work to be done in developing many more conceptions of set, and thinking about their relationships to philosophical questions. We should start broadening our horizons *now*.

10.4 Potentialism, Actualism, and Absolute Generality

Throughout this Element, we've been discussing modal theories of sets. An important question in the philosophy of mathematics concerns how we should think of these modalities. I want to put on the table three possible answers to this question:

Actualism/Universism There is a single universe of sets and a definite plurality of all sets.

Potentialism There is a single universe of sets, but it is modally indefinite. There is no definite plurality of all sets.

Multiversism There is no single universe of all sets, rather many universes.

(**Note:** It may be that we should relativise these questions to a given conception, with different questions of how the stages/worlds/modalities are interpreted for different conceptions.)

These views do not exhaust the logical space (e.g. we could have a universe that is indefinite, but not modally so; see Feferman (2010), Scambler (2020)) but they are the main ones that are relevant for iterative conceptions. Each view suggests a different way of philosophically interpreting the relevant modalities. Let's start with the modalities involved in the theories we've considered. The actualist regards the use of modality as a mere heuristic for talking about the stage-theoretic structure of the universe. The potentialist takes the modality seriously, and thinks that it is somehow indicative of the fundamental nature of reality. The multiversist also thinks that the modality is a mere heuristic but in a very different way from the actualist; for them it is a way of talking about interrelationships between the different universes on offer, and ways of moving between them.

Each view has its own idiosyncrasies and suite of problems to be addressed. One aspect of each is how we regard the *determinacy of truth* concerning mathematical claims (in particular in the language of set theory). The universist will likely assert that every sentence of set theory has a definite truth value – assuming we can refer to their universe without issue, the truth or falsity of claims should just be understood as the truth or falsity of claims there. Likewise the multiversist will likely assert that there are set-theoretic claims of indeterminate truth value – true in some worlds and false in others. The potentialist (given mirroring) is likely to fall on the side of determinacy, at least insofar as 'normal' mathematical claims go (which should be understood under the potentialist translation). Whilst this is perhaps somewhat broad-brush – there are possibilities for modifying the conception of truth for each view – those at least seem like the main options.

For the universist, there is also the old problem of the nature of proper classes. For example, Øystein Linnebo (2010) writes:

> Since a set is completely characterized by its elements, any plurality ... seems to provide a complete and precise characterization of a set .... What more could be needed for such a set to exist?[107] (p. 147)

The problem is as follows. Given the stages of any version of the weak iterative conception, the universist holds that there is a determinate totality of all the sets in the stages. This can be cashed out in plural terms; there are some sets xx such that that could be no set of all the xx (for ease, let's just assume that the xx comprise every pure set). But what is it then that stops us forming these sets into a new set? We have a definite plurality of them, and so could characterise the relevant membership relation. One response is to say that contradiction would ensue. But this only holds if you *assume* that the xx contain every possible pure set. So, the universist has to come up with a meaningful explanation of proper classes that makes it clear why they're different from sets, and why the seeming ability to talk about such collections isn't an issue.

Similarly, many see the generality and flexibility of forcing as evidence that a given domain of sets can be expanded. Here's Hamkins (2012) on the subject:

> A stubborn geometer might insist – like an exotic-travelogue writer who never actually ventures west of seventh avenue – that only Euclidean geometry is real and that all the various non-Euclidean geometries are merely curious simulations within it. Such a position is self-consistent, although stifling, for it appears to miss out on the geometrical insights that can arise from the other modes of reasoning. Similarly, a set theorist with the universe view can insist on an absolute background universe ..., regarding all forcing extensions and other models as curious complex simulations within it. (I have personally witnessed the necessary contortions for class forcing.) Such a perspective may be entirely self-consistent, and I am not arguing that the universe view is incoherent, but rather, my point is that if one regards all outer models of the universe as merely simulated inside it via complex formalisms, one may miss out on insights that could arise from the simpler philosophical attitude taking them as fully real. (p. 426)

So, an open question for the universist is how we should interpret the use of forcing *over the universe* (including how natural these interpretations are).[108]

As noted earlier, the multiversist faces no such difficulties. However, they find themselves in hot water concerning the usual problems of generality

---

[107] Linnebo (2010) is especially concerned with the semantics of *plural* quantification here, and I've suppressed this detail for clarity.

[108] This is a literature I've contributed to in Barton (2021) and Antos et al. (2021).

relativism. They assert that there is no absolute universe, but then immediately seem to make claims about *all* universes. The immediate question is: "Why can't we just understand this domain as the absolute universe?". Since the literature here is *enormous*, I'll say no more about it, but merely point out that it remains open.[109]

The potentialist does not face these problems. If one believes that one can always **Reify!** and **Generify!** over any definite plurality, and talk about these processes modally, one does not face the same difficulties. Any definite plurality forms a set, and any definite plurality can be forced over.[110] Since the universe is not modally definite, they may contend that there is no definite plurality of all sets that could be **Reified!** into a set, and no necessarily uncountable partial orders that could be fed into **Generify!**. This is the response of both Linnebo (2010) (for proper classes only) and Scambler (2021) (for both). *Given that their modality is legitimate*, a response can be made out along these lines. An important question is thus whether that modality can be given an acceptable gloss, or is parasitic on other (unavailable) notions.[111] The multiversist and universist can both explain the modality by reducing it to other notions (direct quantification over universes for the former, restricted quantification over the stages for the latter). So there is a real question of whether the potentialist has just exchanged one suite of problems for another, and whether one is especially worse.

A final question regarding absolute generality concerns the similarity between the reasoning involved in Cantor–Russell and Cohen–Scott. Some authors have argued that the similarity between the two suggests that if one is a **Reify!** potentialist/multiversist, then one should be a **Generify!** potentialist/multiversist too.[112] Really substantiating this thesis would require a more detailed analysis of the similarities between the two pieces of reasoning, and is an open philosophical problem.

Note: This seems like a difficult issue to address, since any such response will have to distinguish both Cantor–Russell and Cohen–Scott from other kinds of 'diagonal' argument where an 'indefinite extensibility' response is not so attractive (e.g. the halting problem; see Meadows (2015)). I do not see an easy way to answer this question, in particular because it is not clear to me if there

---

[109] For further reading see Rayo and Uzquiano (2006), Florio and Linnebo (2021) (esp. chapter 11), and Studd (2019).

[110] There is a question of whether the motivations for these different positions are satisfactory, see Roberts (MSb).

[111] See Linnebo (2018), chs. 3 and 12 for some discussion.

[112] See Meadows (2015), Scambler (2021), and Builes and Wilson (2022) for discussion.

if there is a sharp characterisation of the notion of *diagonal argument* (perhaps instead it is a more 'family resemblance' concept?).[113]

10.5 Connection to Conceptual Engineering

One salient point to be noted is that what I've argued here is closely linked to *conceptual engineering*. This field concerns itself with the evaluation, design, and implementation of our concepts.[114] There are affinities between what we've discussed here and this literature. For example, Kevin Scharp has argued that our naive concept of truth is inconsistent and should be replaced with two concepts (*ascending truth* and *descending truth*) which validate each direction of the Tarski biconditionals separately, but there is no consistent concept that validates both (Scharp, 2013). There are clear similarities with the way in which **Universality** and **Indefinite Extensibility** can be traded off, and how **Forcing Saturation** conflicts with **Powerset**. There is a natural project here to view these moves in the light of conceptual engineering. Indeed Incurvati (2020) explicitly makes this connection for **Indefinite Extensibility** and **Universality**. So we ask:

Question Should we view the project of trading off features of concepts/conceptions of set as an exercise in conceptual engineering? If so, how should we construe the details?

10.6 Plato and Friends

The next objection comes from the staunch set-theoretic realist/platonist, who thinks that there's just a world of sets 'out there' where every set-theoretic sentence has a definite truth value. Conceptions of set are great and all, but at the end of the day the theories they motivate are either true or false about this universe, and this is the only arbiter of correctness we need. All this talk of theoretical virtues and conceptions of set is a mere red herring.

I don't find this line of argument very persuasive at all. I think the history of set theory, with all its twists and turns, false starts, and possible choice points, indicates that this just isn't a very fruitful way to look at things. To see this, let's grant for the sake of argument that there is such a platonic realm. What should we think of our talk concerning it? There is a pessimistic probabilistic argument available here: Do we really think, out of all the possible conceptions

---

[113] I thank Toby Meadows for some discussion of this point. See also Simmons (1990).
[114] See Chalmers (2020) for a survey.

we might have and all the ways we might have gone and continue to go, that we will really select the 'right' one? I think it entirely possible what we've discussed here is probably a very small snapshot of what is quite a large space. The conceptions we've come across may well just constitute a fraction of all the possible conceptions available to humans and gods. What is the probability (given our lack of perceptual interaction with this universe) that we happen to pick the right conception? I would say low.[115]

One could, as a response, say that we *do* have some sort of perception of the universe of sets. I don't have much to say here, beyond the well-worn point that this seems like mysticism to me. Another option is simply a fatalistic pessimism about our chances. But I see a better way out – to regard the interesting questions as ones concerning what we *do* with our conceptions and the theories they motivate, and how they interact with our knowledge as a whole. This strikes me as an area where we can learn and make progress, rather than simply arguing about whose mystical eye sees the farthest.[116]

10.7 Pluralism?

I've argued that we now find ourselves at a fundamental choice point, do we go with **Forcing Saturation**, **Powerset**, or something else entirely? There is, however, a different option: We might end up in a situation in which the various conceptions perform better with respect to certain criteria and/or in different contexts. It's possible that we might be led to a strong kind of pluralism, where claims using the term "set" need to be relativised to a particular kind of conception in order to be assessed for truth. There's a special challenge for analysing mathematical practice here. Normally (at least within ZFC set theory) the 'spectre' of pluralism does not too radically alter the typing of mathematical objects (e.g. within different theories extending ZFC the reals are always a set). However, here we do have significantly different types – the continuum might be a proper class under the countabilist but a tiny accessible set under the strong iterative conception. To me, it seems philosophically open which route we take, or even if we need to pick *one*. So we ask:

Question What are the prospects for a set-theoretic pluralism arising out of the different conceptions of set discussed here?

---

[115] I also make a version of this argument in more detail in Barton (2022).

[116] This way of thinking has *some* affinities with Penelope Maddy's naturalism (Maddy, 1997), second philosophy (Maddy (2007)), and thin realism (Maddy (2011)). I *perhaps* differ from her in that I think that an appealing underlying conception is more than a mere "useful heuristic" (Maddy (2011), p. 136).

10.8 Not the Final Word

I hope to have convinced the reader that there are a host of interesting philosophical and mathematical questions to be found within contemporary philosophy of set theory. I want to close with a word on the methodology of progress in this field. We can only hope to make serious advances on these issues by thoughtful and meticulous examination of different conceptions. A full study of these problems will thus require a massive effort from historians, philosophers, and sociologists of mathematics, as well as philosophically interested mathematicians, and so there's a real opportunity for collaboration from people working in many fields. Even then though, it's not clear how much control we have over our semantic whims.[117] It may be that significant *set-theoretic activism* is needed in order to get conceptions accepted as legitimate and under consideration. In this way, though mathematics has its own norms and methods of reasoning, the present study suggests a radical *anti-exceptionalism* about mathematics as contiguous with other human endeavours. The future is open and exciting, with a good deal of work to be done in understanding the world(s) of infinite sets.

---

[117] The idea that we don't have much control is advocated by Wilson (2006) and Cappelen (2018).

References

Antos, C., Barton, N., and Friedman, S.-D. (2021). Universism and extensions of *V*. *The Review of Symbolic Logic*, 14(1):112–54.

Arrigoni, T., and Friedman, S.-D. (2013). The Hyperuniverse Program. *Bulletin of Symbolic Logic*, 19(1):77–96.

Bagaria, J. (2005). Natural axioms of set theory and the continuum problem. In *Proceedings of the 12th International Congress of Logic, Methodology, and Philosophy of Science*, pages 43–64. King's College London Publications.

Barton, N. (2017). Executing Gödel's Programme in Set Theory. PhD thesis, Birkbeck, University of London.

Barton, N. (2021). Indeterminateness and 'the' universe of sets: Multiversism, potentialism, and pluralism. In Fitting, M., editor, *Selected Topics from Contemporary Logics*, Landscapes in Logic 2, pages 105–82. College Publications.

Barton, N. (2022). Structural relativity and informal rigour. In Oliveri, G., Ternullo, C., and Boscolo, S., editors, *Objects, Structures, and Logics: FilMat Studies in the Philosophy of Mathematics*, pages 133–74. Springer International Publishing.

Barton, N. (MSa). Is (un)countabilism restrictive? To appear in the *Journal of Philosophical Logic*. Preprint: https://philpapers.org/rec/BARIUR.

Barton, N. (MSb). What makes a 'good' modal theory of sets? Manuscript under review. Preprint: https://philpapers.org/rec/BARWMA-9.

Barton, N., and Friedman, S. (2019). Set theory and structures. In Sarikaya, D., Kant, D., and Centrone, S., editors, *Reflections on the Foundations of Mathematics*, pages 223–53. Springer.

Barton, N., and Friedman, S. (MS). Countabilism and maximality principles. Manuscript under review. Preprint: https://philpapers.org/rec/BARCAM-5.

Barton, N., Müller, M., and Prunescu, M. (2022). On representations of intended structures in foundational theories. *Journal of Philosophical Logic*, 51(2):283–96.

Bell, J. (2011). *Set Theory: Boolean-Valued Models and Independence Proofs*. Oxford University Press.

Bell, J. (2014). *Intuitionistic Set Theory*. Studies in Logic 50. College Publications.

Boolos, G. (1984). To be is to be a value of a variable (or to be some values of some variables). *The Journal of Philosophy*, 81(8):430–49.

Boolos, G. (1998). Reply to Charles Parsons' 'Sets and Classes'. In Richard Jeffrey, editor, *Logic, Logic, and Logic*, pages 30–6. Harvard University Press.

Brauer, E. (MS). What is forcing potentialism? Manuscript under review.

Builes, D., and Wilson, J. M. (2022). In defense of countabilism. *Philosophical Studies*, 179(7):2199–236.

Button, T. (2021a). Level Theory Part 1: Axiomatizing the bare idea of a cumulative hierarchy of sets. *The Bulletin of Symbolic Logic*, 27(4):436–60.

Button, T. (2021b). Level Theory, Part 2: Axiomatizing the bare idea of a potential hierarchy. *Bulletin of Symbolic Logic*, 27(4):461–84.

Button, T. (2022). Level Theory, Part 3: A Boolean algebra of sets arranged in well-ordered levels. *Bulletin of Symbolic Logic*, 28(1):1–26.

Caicedo, A. E., Cummings, J., Koellner, P., and Larson, P. B., editors (2017). *Foundations of Mathematics: Logic at Harvard Essays in Honor of W. Hugh Woodin's 60th Birthday*, volume 690 of Contemporary Mathematics. American Mathematical Society.

Cain, J. (1995). Infinite utility. *Australasian Journal of Philosophy*, 73(3):401–4.

Cappelen, H. (2018). *Fixing Language: An Essay on Conceptual Engineering*. Oxford University Press.

Chalmers, D. J. (2020). What is conceptual engineering and what should it be? *Inquiry*. DOI: https://doi.org/10.1080/0020174X.2020.1817141

Cohen, P. (1963). The independence of the continuum hypothesis. *Proceedings of the National Academy of Sciences of the United States of America*, 50(6):1143–8.

Cohen, P. (2002). The discovery of forcing. *Rocky Mountain Journal of Mathematics*, 32(4):1071–100.

Drake, F. R. (1974). *Set Theory: An Introduction to Large Cardinals*. North Holland Publishing Co.

Drake, F. R. and Singh, D. (1996). *Intermediate Set Theory*. Wiley.

Enderton, H. (1977). *Elements of Set Theory*. Academic Press.

Feferman, S. (2010). On the strength of some semi-constructive set theories. In Berger, U., Diener, H., Schuster, P., and Seisenberger, M., editors, *Logic, Construction, Computation*, pp. 201–226. De Gruyter.

Feferman, S., Friedman, H., Maddy, P., and Steel, J. (2000). Does mathematics need new axioms? *Bulletin of Symbolic Logic*, 6(4):401–46.

Feferman, S., and Hellman, G. (1995). Predicative foundations of arithmetic. *Journal of Philosophical Logic*, 24(1):1–17.

Ferreirós, J. (2007). *Labyrinth of Thought: A History of Set Theory and Its Role in Modern Mathematics (2nd Edition)*. Springer, Birkhäuser.

Fine, K. (2005). Class and membership. *Journal of Philosophy*, 102(11):547–72.

Florio, S., and Leach-Krouse, G. (2017). What Russell should have said to Burali-Forti. *Review of Symbolic Logic*, 10(4):682–718.

Florio, S., and Linnebo, O. (2021). *The Many and the One: A Philosophical Study of Plural Logic*. Oxford University Press.

Forster, T. (2008). The iterative conception of set. *The Review of Symbolic Logic*, 1(1):97–110.

Geschke, S., and Quickert, S. (2004). On Sacks forcing and the Sacks property. In Löwe, B., Piwinger, B., and Räsch, T., editors, *Classical and New Paradigms of Computation and their Complexity Hierarchies*, pages 95–139, Springer Netherlands.

Giaquinto, M. (2002). *The Search for Certainty: A Philosophical Account of Foundations of Mathematics*. Oxford University Press.

Gitman, V., Hamkins, J. D., and Johnstone, T. A. (2016). What is the theory ZFC without power set? *Mathematical Logic Quarterly*, 62(4–5):391–406.

Gödel, K. (1940). *The Consistency of the Continuum Hypothesis*. Princeton University Press.

Gödel, K. (1947). What is Cantor's continuum problem? In *[Gödel, 1990]*, pages 176–87. Oxford University Press.

Gödel, K. (1964). What is Cantor's continuum problem? In *[Gödel, 1990]*, pages 254–70. Oxford University Press.

Gödel, K. (1990). *Collected Works, Volume II: Publications 1938–1974*. Oxford University Press. Edited by: Solomon Feferman (Editor-in-chief), John W. Dawson, Jr., Stephen C. Kleene, Gregory H. Moore, Robert M. Solovay, Jean van Heijenoort.

Goldstein, L. (2012). Paradoxical partners: Semantical brides and set-theoretical grooms. *Analysis*, 73(1):33–7.

Hamkins, J. D. (2012). The set-theoretic multiverse. *The Review of Symbolic Logic*, 5(3):416–49.

Hamkins, J. D. and Lewis, A. (2000). Infinite time Turing machines. *Journal of Symbolic Logic*, 65(2):567–604.

Hamkins, J. D. and Loewe, B. (2008). The modal logic of forcing. *Transactions of the American Mathematical Society*, 360(4):1793–817.

Hamkins, J. D. and Montero, B. (2000). With infinite utility, more needn't be better. *Australasian Journal of Philosophy*, 78(2):231–40.

Holmes, M., Forster, T., and Libert, T. (2012). Alternative set theories. In *Sets and Extensions in the Twentieth Century*, volume 6 of Handbook of the History of Logic, pages 559–632. Elsevier/North-Holland, Amsterdam.

Incurvati, L. (2017). Maximality principles in set theory. *Philosophia Mathematica*, 25(2):159–93.

Incurvati, L. (2020). *Conceptions of Set and the Foundations of Mathematics*. Cambridge University Press.

Incurvati, L. and Murzi, J. (2017). Maximally consistent sets of instances of naive comprehension. *Mind*, 126(502):371–84.

Jockwich, S., Tarafder, S., and Venturi, G. (2022). Ideal objects for set theory. *Journal of Philosophical Logic*, 51(3):583–602.

Kanamori, A. (2007). Gödel and set theory. *The Bulletin of Symbolic Logic*, 13(2):153–88.

Kanamori, A. (2009). *The Higher Infinite: Large Cardinals in Set Theory from Their Beginnings*. Springer, 2nd edition.

Koellner, P. (2009). On reflection principles. *Annals of Pure and Applied Logic*, 157(2–3):206–19.

Koellner, P. (2014). Large cardinals and determinacy. In Zalta, E. N., editor, *The Stanford Encyclopedia of Philosophy*. Metaphysics Research Lab, Stanford University, spring 2014 edition.

Krapf, R. (2017). *Class forcing and second-order arithmetic*. PhD thesis, The University of Bonn. Universitäts- und Landesbibliothek Bonn.

Kunen, K. (1980). *Set Theory: An Introduction to Independence Proofs*. Elsevier.

Kunen, K. (2013). *Set Theory*. College Publications.

Linnebo, Ø. (2006). Sets, properties, and unrestricted quantification. In Rayo, A., and Uzquiano, G., editors, *Absolute Generality*, pages 149–78, Oxford University Press.

Linnebo, Ø. (2010). Pluralities and sets. *Journal of Philosophy*, 107(3):144–64.

Linnebo, Ø. (2013). The potential hierarchy of sets. *The Review of Symbolic Logic*, 6(2):205–28.

Linnebo, Ø. (2014). Plural quantification. In Zalta, E. N., editor, *The Stanford Encyclopedia of Philosophy*. Fall 2014 edition.

Linnebo, Ø. (2018). *Thin Objects: An Abstractionist Account*. Oxford University Press.

Linnebo, Ø., and Shapiro, S. (2023). Predicativism as a form of potentialism. *Review of Symbolic Logic*, 16(1):1–32.

Mac Lane, S. (1986). *Mathematics: Form and Function*. Springer.

Maddy, P. (1983). Proper classes. *Journal of Symbolic Logic*, 48(1):113–19.

Maddy, P. (1988a). Believing the axioms I. *The Journal of Symbolic Logic*, 53(2):481–511.

Maddy, P. (1988b). Believing the axioms II. *The Journal of Symbolic Logic*, 53(3):736–64.

Maddy, P. (1997). *Naturalism in Mathematics*. Oxford University Press.

Maddy, P. (2007). *Second Philosophy*. Oxford University Press.

Maddy, P. (2011). *Defending the Axioms*. Oxford University Press.

Maddy, P. (2017). Set-theoretic foundations. In *[Caicedo et al., 2017]*, pages 289–322. American Mathematical Society.

Maddy, P. (2019). What Do We Want a Foundation to Do?, pages 293–311, in Centrone, S., Kant, D., and Sarikaya, D., editors, *Reflections on the Foundations of Mathematics*. Synthese Library, vol. 407. Springer International Publishing, Cham.

Maddy, P., and Meadows, T. (2020). A reconstruction of Steel's multiverse project. *The Bulletin of Symbolic Logic*, 26(2):118–69.

Mancosu, P. (2009). Measuring the size of infinite collections of natural numbers: Was Cantor's theory of infinite number inevitable? *Review of Symbolic Logic*, 2(4):612–46.

Meadows, T. (2015). Naive infinitism. *Notre Dame Journal of Formal Logic*, 56(1):191–212.

Menzel, C. (1986). On the iterative explanation of the paradoxes. *Philosophical Studies*, 49(1):37–61.

Menzel, C. (2014). *ZFCU*, wide sets, and the iterative conception. *Journal of Philosophy*, 111(2):57–83.

Menzel, C. (2021). Modal set theory. In Bueno, O. and Shalkowski, S. A., editors, *The Routledge Handbook of Modality*, pages 292–307. Routledge.

Moore, A. W. (1990). *The Infinite*. Routledge.

Moore, J. T. (2010). The proper forcing axiom. In *Proceedings of the International Congress of Mathematicians 2010 (ICM 2010)*, pages 3–29.

Muller, F. A. (2001). Sets, classes and categories. *British Journal for the Philosophy of Science*, 52:539–73.

Oliver, A., and Smiley, T. (2013). *Plural Logic*. Oxford University Press.

Parker, M. W. (2019). Gödel's argument for Cantorian Cardinality. *Noûs*, 53(2):375–93.

Parsons, C. (1983). Sets and modality. In *Mathematics in Philosophy: Selected Essays*, pages 298–342. Cornell University Press.

Posy, C. J. (2020). *Mathematical Intuitionism*. Elements in the Philosophy of Mathematics. Cambridge University Press.

Potter, M. (2004). *Set Theory and Is Philosophy: A Critical Introduction*. Oxford University Press.

Priest, G. (2002). *Beyond the Limits of Thought*. Clarendon Press.

Quine, W. (1937). New foundations for mathematical logic. *The American Mathematical Monthly*, 44(2):70–80.

Rayo, A., and Uzquiano, G., editors (2006). *Absolute Generality*. Clarendon Press.

Reinhardt, W. (1974). Remarks on reflection principles, large cardinals, and elementary embeddings. *Proceedings of Symposia in Pure Mathematics*, 13(2):189–205.

Rittberg, C. J. (2020). *Mathematical Practices Can Be Metaphysically Laden*, pages 1–26. Springer International Publishing. DOI: https://doi.org/10.1007/978-3-030-19071-2_22-1

Roberts, S. (2016). *Reflection and Potentialism*. PhD thesis, Birkbeck, University of London.

Roberts, S. (2019). Modal structuralism and reflection. *The Review of Symbolic Logic*, 12(4):823–60.

Roberts, S. (2022). Pluralities as nothing over and above. *Journal of Philosophy*, 119(8):405–24.

Roberts, S. (MSa). The iterative conception of properties. Unpublished manuscript.

Roberts, S. (MSb). Ultimate *V*. Manuscript under review. Preprint: https://philarchive.org/rec/ROBUVS.

Scambler, C. (2020). An indeterminate universe of sets. *Synthese*, 197(2):545–73.

Scambler, C. (2021). Can all things be counted? *Journal of Philosophical Logic*, 50: 1079–106.

Scambler, C. (MS). On the consistency of height and width potentialism. Manuscript under review.

Scharp, K. (2013). *Replacing Truth*. Oxford University Press.

Scott, D. (1977). Foreword to *Boolean-Valued Models and Independence Proofs*. In *[Bell, 2011]*, pages xiii–xviii. Oxford University Press.

Shapiro, S. and Wright, C. (2006). All things indefinitely extensible. In Rayo, A. and Uzquiano, G., editors, *Absolute Generality*, pages 255–304. Oxford University Press.

Simmons, K. (1990). The diagonal argument and the liar. *Journal of Philosophical Logic*, 19(3):277–303.

Skolem, T. (1922). Some remarks on axiomitized set theory. In *A Source Book in Mathematical Logic, 1879–1931, van Heijenoort 1967*, pages 290–301. Harvard University Press.

Solovay, R. M. (1974). On the cardinality of Σ_2^1 sets of reals. *Journal of Symbolic Logic*, 39(2):330–330.

Steel, J. (2014). Gödel's program. In Kennedy, J., editor, *Interpreting Gödel*, pp. 153–179. Cambridge University Press.

Studd, J. P. (2013). The iterative conception of set: A (bi-) modal axiomatisation. *Journal of Philosophical Logic*, 42(5):697–725.

Studd, J. P. (2019). *Everything, More or Less: A Defence of Generality Relativism*. Oxford University Press.

Taranovsky, D. (2004). Perfect subset property for co-analytic sets in ZF\P. Online article: https://web.mit.edu/dmytro/www/other/Perfect SubsetsAndZFC.htm.

Uzquiano, G. (2006). Unrestricted unrestricted quantification: The cardinal problem of absolute generality. In *Absolute Generality*, pages 305–32. Oxford University Press.

Weaver, N. (2014). *Forcing for Mathematicians*. World Scientific.

Whittle, B. (2015). On infinite size. *Oxford Studies in Metaphysics*, 9:3–19.

Whittle, B. (2018). Size and function. *Erkenntnis*, 83(4):853–73.

Wilson, M. (2006). *Wandering Significance: An Essay on Conceptual Behaviour*. Oxford University Press.

Woodin, W. H. (2017). In search of Ultimate-*L*: The 19th Midrasha Mathematicae lectures. *The Bulletin of Symbolic Logic*, 23(1):1–109.

Zarach, A. M. (1996). *Replacement ↛ collection*, volume 6 of Lecture Notes in Logic, pages 307–22. Springer.

Acknowledgements

This short Element came to be as a result of a lot of help from a lot of different people. My intellectual debts are great, and any list of thanks is going to be very incomplete. Constraints of space prevent me from going on as long as I would like. But it's still good to try.

I got excellent comments on drafts from Salvatore Florio, Marcus Giaquinto, Sigurd Jorem, Julie Lauvsland, Øystein Linnebo, Toby Meadows, Sam Roberts, Chris Scambler, Zeynep Soysal, Davide Sutto, Sofie Vaas, Mahan Vaz, Pascal Wagner, and Daniel Waxman, as well as two anonymous reviewers for Cambridge University Press. I thank all of you heartily for your time, patience, and helpfulness.

In addition, there are many people with whom I have had very useful conversations regarding ideas behind the text, and whose words helped shape the Element. I can remember having especially fruitful interactions with Carolin Antos, Joan Bagaria, Robert Black, Tim Button, Laura Crosilla, Raphaël Carroy, Neil Dewar, Alexander Douglas, Monroe Eskew, Juliet Floyd, Sy-David Friedman, Victoria Gitman, Olav Gjelsvik, Joel-David Hamkins, Luca Incurvati, Akihiro Kanamori, Daniel Kuby, Maxwell Levine, Penelope Maddy, Beau Madison Mount, Rupert McCallum, Colin McLarty, Sandra Müller, Michael Potter, Agustín Rayo, Ian Rumfitt, Ethan Russo, Jeffrey Schatz, Stewart Shapiro, Robin Solberg, James Studd, Fenner Tanswell, Philip Welch, and Kameryn J. Williams. My apologies to the large number of people whom I have forgotten.

Versions of this work were presented at University of Oslo, University of Konstanz, University of California, Davis, and the National University of Singapore. I thank those audiences for their input.

I would like also to thank Penny Rush and Stewart Shapiro for their editorial work and for bringing together the Elements in the Philosophy of Mathematics series. Shalini Bisa and Hilary Gaskin were very patient and helpful with the administrative side of things, and I thank them for their hard work.

I've been very lucky to be part of some great institutions. Birkbeck provided a fantastic place to do my graduate work. The Kurt Gödel Research Center for Mathematical Logic was a hive of logical activity whilst I was there. Konstanz was both a very supportive and energetic place to do philosophy. And though I haven't been there long, I'm having a great time in Oslo and enjoying myself immensely.

I'm grateful also for the financial support of the UK Arts and Humanities Research Council whilst doing my PhD, the FWF (Austrian Science Fund) during my stay in Vienna, the VolswagenStiftung whilst I was in Konstanz, and Norges Forskningsrådet (Research Council of Norway) who provide my current funding.

I owe much to my partner Nikki. She's been a constant source of inspiration, and if this Element holds up halfway to the standards she sets for herself, I'll be very happy.

Lastly, I dedicate this Element to my parents Jeanne and Paul, who have supported my curiosity for as long as I can remember.

Acknowledgements

Cambridge Elements ≡

The Philosophy of Mathematics

Penelope Rush
University of Tasmania

From the time Penny Rush completed her thesis in the philosophy of mathematics (2005), she has worked continuously on themes around the realism/anti-realism divide and the nature of mathematics. Her edited collection *The Metaphysics of Logic* (Cambridge University Press, 2014), and forthcoming essay 'Metaphysical Optimism' (*Philosophy Supplement*), highlight a particular interest in the idea of reality itself and curiosity and respect as important philosophical methodologies.

Stewart Shapiro
The Ohio State University

Stewart Shapiro is the O'Donnell Professor of Philosophy at The Ohio State University, a Distinguished Visiting Professor at the University of Connecticut, and a Professorial Fellow at the University of Oslo. His major works include *Foundations without Foundationalism* (1991), *Philosophy of Mathematics: Structure and Ontology* (1997), *Vagueness in Context* (2006), and *Varieties of Logic* (2014). He has taught courses in logic, philosophy of mathematics, metaphysics, epistemology, philosophy of religion, Jewish philosophy, social and political philosophy, and medical ethics.

About the Series

This Cambridge Elements series provides an extensive overview of the philosophy of mathematics in its many and varied forms. Distinguished authors will provide an up-to-date summary of the results of current research in their fields and give their own take on what they believe are the most significant debates influencing research, drawing original conclusions.

The Philosophy of Mathematics

Elements in the Series

A full series listing is available at: www.cambridge.org/EPM